*Alex
Enjoy this Book
Sept 3rd 2023
Fr. T. White*

P.R.A.Y.

Building a
**Purposeful
Relationship** between
Abba and
Yourself

REVEREND SHARON DUNN

 FriesenPress

One Printers Way
Altona, MB R0G 0B0
Canada

www.friesenpress.com

Copyright © 2023 by Reverend Sharon Dunn
First Edition — 2023

All rights reserved.

No part of this publication may be reproduced in any form, or by any means, electronic or mechanical, including photocopying, recording, or any information browsing, storage, or retrieval system, without permission in writing from FriesenPress.

ISBN
978-1-03-917829-8 (Hardcover)
978-1-03-917828-1 (Paperback)
978-1-03-917830-4 (eBook)

1. RELIGION, PRAYER

Distributed to the trade by The Ingram Book Company

Table of Contents

Acknowledgments 1

Introduction 3

Chapter 1: Man Should Always Pray, and Not Faint 9

Chapter 2: Prayer is a Command to the Body of Christ 17

Chapter 3: We Pray to Make Our Requests and Petitions Known 27

Chapter 4: Praying the Will of God in Your Circumstances
(The Lord's Prayer) 35

Chapter 5: We Pray for Growth and Transformation 42

Chapter 6: We Do Warfare in Prayer 51

Chapter 7: Hindrances to Prayer 60

Chapter 8: The Power of Thought 69

Chapter 9: Generational Curses and Self-Deliverance 84

Chapter 10: Disobedience and Deliverance 94

Chapter 11: The Last Will and Testament of Jesus Christ 111

Chapter 12: Come into Agreement with God 119

Chapter 13: Praying the Word of God 125

Conclusion 137

About the Author 141

Acknowledgments

I AM GRATEFUL for my family, who God has blessed me with. My son Donald, my daughter Natasha and her family, my son Nathan and his family, and my daughter Danielle and her family. Thank you for your love and support.

Words cannot express my gratitude to my dear sister who has given her time and creativity to edit this book. Thank you, Michelle.

I am also grateful to the family of God TPCOG and RFCC who have been a support to me in ministry.

How can I say thanks to the One who has stood by me through life's journey? He has been my doctor, my counsellor, my defender, and my friend. He is everything I hope for, and even more. My life is not without struggles, but God has always been there for me. My life belongs to Him. I love the Lord with everything within me. This book would not have been possible without Him. I praise and acknowledge Him as my King and Lord.

Introduction

MANY PEOPLE TODAY are battling disappointment in leadership in the Kingdom of God. There is injustice in the world like never before. It is becoming more and more difficult for believers to discern the true men and women of God. There are some wearing cloaks who appear to be Christ-like, but their true motive is to deceive the body of Christ, leading them away from Jesus to themselves. Many are using their tongues to kill the character of others in God's Kingdom. The Word is being preached with man-made theology mixed in. Not many seem to recognize the conflicting statements that are coming from the pulpits of Western churches, which leaves us to ponder, is God still speaking?

> *"Look, I stand at the door and knock. If you hear my voice and open the door, I will come in and we will share a meal together as friends."*[1]

The church body must have a listening ear to hear what Jesus is saying. He is coming back for the church that

---

1   Revelation 3:20 (New Living Translation)

He loves and died for. This is the time when you need to hear from God for yourself. All of us have the privilege to become sons and daughters of Christ. This gives us the birthright to say "Abba, Father"[2] when we pray. Your relationship with God is what will keep you in these days that we are living in. The world is changing faster than we are able to understand it. Your trust must be completely in God.

The church of God has been under attack from the beginning of time. Jesus said we must take the Kingdom back by force. Separate yourself from the world, learn the devices of Satan's kingdom, and be persistent in the things of God, or you may be deceived. Yes, it is possible for people of God to be in the church and be deceived.

> *"When will this happen? the disciples asked Him later as He sat on the slopes of the Mount of Olives. What events will signal your return and the end of the world? Jesus told them, don't let anyone fool you. For many will come claiming to be the Messiah and will lead many astray."*[3]

Another translation[4] reads, "For many shall come in my name, saying, I am the Christ; and shall deceive many." "Christ" means "anointed one." And indeed, many people today are saying they are anointed by God to do what they

---

2   Galatians 4:6, Romans 8:15 (King James Version)
3   Matthew 24:3–5 (The Living Bible)
4   (KJV)

are doing and that they came to represent Christ, as Jesus said they would, but He gives instruction in verse four above, "...don't let anyone fool you."

Those who are standing for the truth are coming under fire. For everyone who attends church, the opportunity exists to get hurt, be offended, or become angry. No one is exempt, including the person who is preaching the Word of God. We must become mature in our faith and stop using our offense as an excuse to stay away from the House of God. Sometimes, the truth hurts.

These days, people want to hear motivational messages in church rather than the truth. Believers want a license to do whatever they want, with no consequences for their actions. Often this is the result of being hurt by others or is due to a lack of spiritual maturity. The believer, not wanting to hear the truth, may then go from church to church hoping to find what they are looking for and if they don't find it, become hurt and feel betrayed. If they do not find healing, they will eventually hurt and betray others as they go from place to place and become the very thing that they despise. Prayer keeps us alert to the Holy Spirit as He speaks to our conscience.

You have to position yourself and be available to the Holy Spirit to mature you. God is raising up a company of people these days who are called His sons and daughters, who will subdue evil and the kingdom of darkness. For this reason, you were put into this century at this time. God has designed you to accomplish His will. Everything about you was created to influence those around you.

> *"And He has made from one blood every nation of men to dwell on all the face of the earth, and has determined their pre-appointed times and the boundaries of their dwellings, so that they should seek the Lord in the hope that they might grope for Him and find Him, though He is not far from each one of us; for in Him we live and move and have our being as also some of your own poets have said, 'For we are also His offspring.'"*[5]

God knew everything about us while we were still in our mother's womb. He knew where we were going to be born, live, and who our parents would be. He knew what we would be doing today, right now. He gives us the means (the Holy Spirit) to understand the times that we are living in. We are in the days of the true prophets where God is bringing correction and direction to His church. It is not just about prophesying. Prophesy gives edification, exultation, and encouragement. The church also needs correction and direction so that the body of Christ can be edified.

If the trumpet does not give a clear sound, how will the church know who to fight, and when? God has a time and a season for everything. This means spending time with the Lord, learning to know Him and abiding consistently in Him. Only by spending time in the Word of God and prayer, are you able to know His ways. Prayer is like the air we breathe. Air gives oxygen to our blood cells to keep

---

[5] Acts 17:26–28 (New King James Version)

us alive. Likewise, prayer keeps our relationship with the Lord alive.

We obey Jesus' command when we pray. Open communication develops a relationship with God. Doing this daily is following in Jesus' footsteps. When you start talking with the Lord it may begin with just five minutes a day and before you know it, your conversation will go into hours. In the Book of Psalms, you'll find helpful examples of how to pray.[6] I hope that by the end of this book you will understand how important it is to have a close relationship with the Lord and that it will provide you with some guidance on how to enrich and enhance your prayer time with God.

---

6 Psalm 51, Psalm 91, Psalm 23, Psalm 21(KJV)

PRAYER

Father, I pray that the person who has opened this book will understand biblical truths. I pray that intuition and emotion will not become the definition of what is true. Let your word flow freely through their heart. Let the eyes of their understanding be enlightened, and let them know what the hope of their calling is in You. Help them to know what the riches of the glory of their inheritance is in Christ Jesus. Father, let this person know the power of Jesus' resurrection and the fellowship of His sufferings and be made conformable unto His death so that their life can be transformed into the image of Christ. Let them be able to stand perfect and complete in the will of God for their life so that they can become free from strongholds in their life. Break off from their life any limitations and restrictions placed upon them by sin. Let your love abound more and more in their heart so that they can be at peace in your kingdom. In Jesus' Name. Amen. 🙏

Chapter 1

Man Should Always Pray, and Not Faint

I WAS ON my way to work one day, traveling by bus. All of the seats were occupied, so I stood. All of a sudden, the bus seemed to speed up. The next thing I knew, I heard people asking me if I was alright. I was on the floor! I was not aware of how I ended up there, and I can't tell you what happened in the seconds that I was out. After I was helped to my feet, I realized that I had fainted. When you faint you are in the hands of someone else because you don't know what is going on around you.

As this is in the natural world, so it is in the spiritual. The child of God is called to always pray and not to faint. When you don't exercise a prayer lifestyle you have fainted. This gives the evil one control in areas of your life that you are not giving attention to. Praying enforces what Jesus has done on the cross for you and builds your relationship with God. Prayer is talking to Him. It takes time to build this relationship, but it is never too late. Jesus is always at your heart's door waiting for you to open it.

Prayer influences God, but it does not change the plans that He has had from the beginning. It influences God's actions, but not His purpose. When we know God's purpose and pray, according to His will, we give Him the opportunity to act. It is then that we can see the manifestation of God's promises come to pass.

The Holy Spirit inspires direction and releases the power of God into our circumstance. We have the Bible to keep us in sound doctrine. When we digest the Word of God, the Holy Spirit speaks to our spirit, and when we listen to His direction, we are able to pray according to God's will. When we speak God's Word into a situation, under the direction of the Holy Spirit, it is always effective. God's Word has the ability to bring forth life.

When you are in doubt, always go to the Bible to see what God says about what you are praying about. His Word always brings forth fruit; it is never dormant.

We the believers are the church, the body of Christ Jesus. As Ezekiel was called to speak over the dry bones of Israel, we are called to decree the Word of God over our situation. Try to find scripture verses that are compatible with the things that you are praying about, and pray in the Spirit.

"Praying always with all prayer and supplication in the Spirit, being watchful to this end with all perseverance and supplication for all the saints."[7] Just because God is

---

7 Ephesians 6:18 (KJV)

sovereign does not mean that He is always in control of everything that happens in the world. There is a human factor in all of this. Man has made decisions that have caused—and continue to bring about—calamities, such as the downfall of government systems, death, destruction, wars, sickness, homelessness, and many other atrocities. In prayer, God warns or alerts us to Satan's plan, and the Holy Spirit gives us direction of what to pray for. This is why prayers of all kind, for example, warfare, for the sick, intercessory, for protection, etc., are so important. We must devote ourselves to prayer, receiving direction from the Holy Spirit, as well as with supplication.

Protection from the enemy's attack is not automatic. God gave Man free will. We must intentionally use our free will to pray and ask God to intervene in our families, communities, and countries. We also cannot forget to worship the Lord by giving thanks in appreciation for what He has done, for what He is doing, and for what He will do in the future.

We have policemen and security guards to protect our streets, cities, and nations. In the same way, we need watchmen in the body of Christ. Believers need to stand guard spiritually, watching over everything.

Children of God, we are not only praying for His will to be done on Earth, but we are also watching over the church. Why, you may ask? We are looking for the wolves in sheep's clothing; those who pretend to be believers of Christ but will deceive many. We are called to be like soldiers. A good soldier is watchful and well informed about his enemy. He trains and studies everything about his adversary so that he can be effective when he has to go to war. He is a skilled warrior, ready at all times to defend his country. A good soldier does not want to go to war but knows he must when it is necessary.

This is one of the reasons Jesus said, "Men ought always to pray, and not to faint."[8] Just as it is in the natural world, so it is in the spiritual. The believer must be ready at all times to pray God's will be done on Earth as it is in Heaven. If we had more alert and watchful believers praying in the body of Christ, there would be less casualties in the House of God; especially among the leaders. The enemy often targets and entices those in positions of authority to disobey God because he knows that once he gets to them, those who are under the leaders' influence will fall as well.

We must come to the place where we put our trust in God, not Man. It is easy to trust leaders who are men and women of God and to get lost in the idea of their call to ministry. Some leaders may feel that because they have been called to ministry, they are infallible. This is a trap of the enemy. All have sinned and come short of the glory of God. No person is without sin. All of us need the help of the Holy Spirit to live a life that is pleasing to God.

Leaders are there to guide us to Christ, and not to themselves, as that is idolatry. God works through leaders, but we must remember to look to Him first in all areas of our lives, and not to a person.

---

8 Luke 18:1 (KJV)

People get so disappointed and offended when leaders fall into sin, forgetting that the person is only human. We are called Christians because we follow Christ, not Man.

God is waiting to hear from you. You are here for a purpose. One of your purposes is to be an intercessor. Pray over your family, your community, and your country so that God can intervene in every situation. Let me tell you a secret. Jesus prayed for you and I a long time ago.

> *"I am praying not only for these disciples, but also for all who will ever believe in Me through their message. I pray that they will all be one just as You and I are one - as You are in Me Father and I am in You. And may they be in us so that the world will believe You sent Me."*[9]

Everyone has a purpose in life. We do not know everything. We just have to put our trust in the One who knows the future. You may be the only believer in your family, which means you are the one God has chosen to be a gatekeeper for them. If your life is coming under fire by the enemy, continue to pray. The enemy knows you are the one God is using to break your family's strongholds. We need to put on the whole armour of God so that we can stand against Satan's tricks.

I have seen the results that praying can have against the enemy's plan for my family members. I have experienced victory time and time again as I have labored in prayer to

---

9 John 17:20–1 (TLB)

see the will of God done in my family. You do not have to live in fear, depression, or in lack of anything. Pray about every aspect of your life. It does not matter how small it is, God is interested in everything about you. He knows that you have everyday needs. He is a good Father. Do not take my word for it, pray, and see what happens. Some situations will take time before you see results. Do not get discouraged. Have faith, and be patient.

God works through the prayers of His people, but our human nature is always warring against God's purpose for our lives. When we want to do the right thing, the wrong ideas come to mind. The truth is, as we build intimacy with God in prayer, we will begin to see things from His perspective.

Jesus did not leave us defenseless. He died on the cross for our sins. There was an exchange that took place when Jesus was crucified. He took our sin and gave us His righteousness. When we come to God in prayer, it's not about us being right in ourselves but about what Jesus did on the cross for us. Jesus is representing us before the Father, sinless, as if we had never sinned. Whenever the believer comes before God, Jesus is always there, saying to the Father, "Listen to him, listen to her, I paid the debt."

Now we no longer have to do penance. Reconciliation was achieved when we received salvation. You must believe wholeheartedly that you are redeemed from sin when you receive salvation. As you pray, have faith and believe that God is listening to you, hearing every word you are saying.

> *"But without faith, it is impossible to please Him, for he who comes to God must believe that He is, and that He is a rewarder of those who diligently seek Him."[10]*

Prayer must be done in faith. You must believe in the One that you are praying to. A child of God must believe that not only does the true God exist, but He also rewards your faith in Him. Nothing is able to separate you from the love of God. He showed us His great love when Christ died on the cross for our sins. When you are confident that God loves you, you are able to come before Him boldly. All have sinned and come short of the glory of God and need His grace. The eyes of the Lord are on the believers, and His ear is open to their crying. Take a leap of faith and know that God hears you when you pray.

> *"Now this is the confidence that we have in Him, that if we ask anything according to His will, He hears us. And if we know that He hears us, whatever we ask, we know that we have the petition that we have asked of Him."[11]*

Know with absolute assurance that God will answer your prayer when you ask, according to His will.

---

10   Hebrews 11:6 (NKJV)
11   1 John 5:14–15 (NKJV)

PRAISE BREAK
Psalm 145:2
Every day I will bless You, and I will praise your name, forever and ever. I will praise you at all times.

PRAYER
Father, reveal Yourself to me as I read your Word. Keep me from all evil. Let your truths have free access in my life, and strengthen my inner being with might by Your Spirit. I ask for understanding to pray your will in every area of my life. In Jesus' Name. Amen. 🙏

TAKE AWAY
- Men should always pray, and not faint.
- When you pray, believe that God is listening to you, hearing every word you are saying

Chapter 2

Prayer is a Command to the Body of Christ

PRAYER IS LIKE the air we breathe. Air gives oxygen to the blood cells to keep us alive. Likewise, prayer keeps the believer's relationship with the Lord alive. When we pray, we obey Jesus' command. Jesus is the Son of God, yet prayer was an important part of His life. His disciples saw results when He prayed, so they asked Him to teach them to pray.[12]

Daily prayer opens the eyes of the believer's understanding and helps us to see things from God's perspective. Prayer is not just for petitions; it transfers power, and it is an authorized spiritual system in the believer's life. In times of prayer, an exchange happens between Divinity and believer. The child of God has to maintain communication with the Father for transformation to take place.

---

12 Luke 11:1 (NKJV)

Daily praying is vital to maintaining a spiritual life and intimacy with God. It is also necessary for victory over temptation. Prayer brings us into fellowship and spiritual growth in Christ. In daily prayer, the believer can bring his petitions and requests to God, and it keeps the believer's faith alive. It gives the believer grace for warfare so that they can intercede for others. God's desire is to transform the believer's life into Christ-likeness. God wants you in a position of authority and dominion over your circumstances. As long as the Holy Spirit is allowed to have control, God can come into that person's circumstances and change it for the better.

> *"But you beloved, building yourselves up on your most holy faith, praying in the Holy Spirit, keep yourselves in the love of God, looking for the mercy of our Lord Jesus Christ unto eternal life."*[13]

There is power in prayer when your desire is God and not things. God does not take anything away from us. We were created in His image and likeness, which enriches our lives. Sin takes joy and peace away from us and can affect the quality of life that we live here on Earth. When you are walking in the light as Jesus is the Light, you will have fellowship with God and know His will for your life.

God established His priority at the beginning of creation; that Man was to have dominion over everything. He made it clear by His own declaration to Adam, that if he

---

13 Jude 20–21 (NKJV)

ate from the tree of good and evil, he would die. When Adam disobeyed God, all of mankind died spiritually and became enemies of God. We are naturally disobedient to God's command. Jesus came to Earth and established God's number one priority for mankind. He said, "Repent, for the Kingdom of Heaven is at hand."[14] We are to seek the Kingdom of God and His righteousness and everything we need will be given to us.[15]

Prayer builds confidence in the Creator's obligation and commitment to sustain the believer. Having knowledge of God's will changes a person's perspective to prioritize and put Him first and know that their basic needs will be met daily.

> *"Now this is the confidence that we have in Him, that if we ask anything according to His will, He hears us. And if we know that He hears us, whatever we ask, we know that we have the petitions that we have asked of Him."*[16]

> *"The effectual fervent prayer of a righteous man avails much."*[17]

When you enter into prayer with a mindset of coming into agreement with God's will, prayer is more meaningful.

---

14 Matthew 3:2 (NKJV)
15 Matthew 6:33 (NIV)
16 1 John 5:14–15 (KJV)
17 James 5:16b (NKJV)

The most powerful motivation in the heart of Man is the pursuit of power. It is the desire to control your environment and circumstances. Man was made in God's image and likeness and was created for dominion.

> *"And God said let us make man in our image, after our likeness and let them have dominion over the fish of the sea and over the fowl of the air and over the cattle and over all the earth and over every creeping thing that creeped upon the earth."*[18]

Man was created to exercise power and designed to manage it. Therefore, there is a natural desire in our hearts to seek power.

There are some basic needs that are common to all people in every culture. Everyone needs food, water, clothes, housing, protection, security, and significance. We often do things that are not right so that we can obtain these needs or "have power" over them. However, Jesus gives the answer to what the heart of Man truly needs.

> *"But seek ye first the kingdom of God, and His righteousness and all these things shall be added unto you."*[19]

To "seek" means to pursue with passion; to be determined to have a desire for something. To be "righteous"

---

18   Genesis 1:26 (KJV)

19   Matthew 6:33 (KJV)

means to be in lawful standing with the government. If the principles of God are kept, He will protect and meet every need. We do not have to do wrong things to obtain power. God will give that power to us freely.

At creation, God gave Man dominion over the entire physical realm, making him the king of the earth. To dominate means to govern, rule, control, manage, lead, and have power or authority over something. The person who is assigned the position of rulership has to take on or maintain the responsibility of that position.

> *"For by Him were all things created, that are in heaven and that are in earth, visible and invisible, whether they be thrones, or dominions, or principalities, or powers: all things were created by Him, and for Him."*[20]

God is King over everything, whether visible or invisible, from His throne in Heaven. There is no vote in the Kingdom of God. His Word is supreme and absolute. God is and will remain the sovereign King. He reigns in glory and majesty over the invisible spirit realm. Yet, in the physical realm, He rules in a different way.

God chose us to exercise His authority on Earth. He gave us power. That is why God set up a qualification program from the beginning. He told Adam that "as long as you obey Me, you will live." God is a Spirit, so when He speaks, His words become law. His integrity will not

---

20 Colossians 1:16 (KJV)

permit Him to violate or break His word. He gave Man dominion over the earth, so we are given the command to pray. Prayerlessness can bring envy, jealousy, unrest, and bitterness into a believer's life and lead to a loss of power and authority in Christ.

When God made Mankind to have dominion over the earth, He imparted to us the ability and desire to govern, rule, lead, and manage. As such, it is Man's nature to resist being ruled or controlled by others. We rebel against authority. We rebel against Man's leadership and, in turn, rebel against God's authority. This was not God's plan for the human race. Our resistance to others ruling over us is due to the leadership ability God placed in us to rule over the earth. We are now experiencing difficulties in life because our environment has changed. Sin changes everything. We live in a world that is filled with lust, pride, greed, and selfish desires. The key to fulfilling your purpose here on Earth is to come into alignment with God's Word; to do His will.

Knowing God's original plan for Man can only happen when we are in a "talking relationship" with Him. When we are in a talking relationship with the Father it becomes easy to do His will. The will of God is revealed in Jesus. Everything Jesus did was an expression of God's will. To understand God's will, you must first understand that there is His permissive will and His perfect will.

The permissive will of God is what has been done in righteousness and within the boundary of God's character. The perfect will of God is what has been revealed in His

Word. The character and will of God are revealed in the Holy Scripture.

An example of God's will regarding God-given authority is shown when Jesus went to John the Baptist to be baptized.

> *"But John forbad Him saying I have need to be baptized of thee, and comest thou to me? And Jesus answering said unto him, suffer it to be so now for thus it becometh us to fulfil all righteousness. Then he suffered him."*[21]

Jesus is the Son of God, yet He went to John to be baptized. According to the law, John the Baptist was in authority at the time. Jesus hadn't begun His ministry yet. He followed the law and submitted to John's authority. This should encourage us to follow in Jesus' footsteps and be obedient to those who are in authority.

Jesus Christ, who was God in the flesh, submitted to the authority He established on the earth.

> *"Submitting to one another out of reverence for Christ."*[22]

We are following the precept of Jesus by being respectful to those who are in authority over us. However, we should not follow men and women into sin. The Bible tells us to

---

21 Matthew 3:14–15 (KJV)
22 Ephesians 5:21 (English Standard Version)

always submit. Submitting is to be respectful in our attitude towards someone. We can be respectful to those in authority and still not obey them if they are operating in sin. It is better to obey God than to disobey Him.

> *"Let every soul be subject unto the higher powers. For there is no power but of God the powers that be ordained of God."*[23]

> *"Neither shall they say, Lo here or lo there! For behold the Kingdom of God is within you."*[24]

The Kingdom of God on Earth is God's authority within the heart of Man. Through the Holy Spirit we take the King with us everywhere we go and impact our environment. Jesus brought the Kingdom with Him and in Him. When the Holy Spirit is inside of us, we too carry His Kingdom wherever we go. The Kingdom of Heaven is where the people of God impact their environment with God-given authority. Jesus said, "Repent, for the Kingdom of Heaven is at hand."[25]

You can have all the facts about Jesus and still not know Him. You can have biblical knowledge without giving yourself totally to the Holy Spirit for Him to regenerate you on the inside. You must come to that place in your

---

23 Romans 13:1 (KJV)
24 Luke 17:21 (KJV)
25 Matthew 3:2 (KJV)

heart where you are persuaded that Jesus is Lord, and He becomes Lord over your life.

> *"And so dear brothers, I plead with you to give your bodies to God. Let them be a living sacrifice holy, the kind He can accept. When you think of what He has done for you, is this too much to ask?"*[26]

We have this invitation to have a personal relationship with the Creator of everything through prayer. What an honor we have as Christians to know God this way. The effectiveness of our prayer will elevate in direct proportion to the depth of our relationship with God.

---
26 Romans 12:1 (TLB)

PRAISE BREAK

Psalm 145:10

All Your works shall praise You, oh Lord, and your saints shall bless you. I bless You, Lord, with my whole heart.

PRAYER

Father, thank You for your grace and mercy. Lord Jesus, create in me the desire to be consistent in prayer. Lead and guide me into a deeper understanding of Your word. Without Your help, I will not be able to obey your command. I need Your grace for each step I take. In Jesus' Name. Amen. 🙏

TAKE AWAY

- Prayer is a command to the body of Christ. Daily praying is vital to maintain a spiritual life and intimacy with God.

Chapter 3

We Pray to Make Our Requests and Petitions Known

PRAYER GIVES YOU a platform to make decrees and spiritual legislation.

> *"Say to them, 'As I live,' says the Lord, 'just as you have spoken in My hearing, so I will do to you...'"*[27]

> *"You will also declare a thing and it will be established for you, so light will shine on your ways."*[28]

This is not to demand things from God, but to come into agreement with Him to carry out His will.

---

27 Numbers 14:28 (NKJV)
28 Job 22:28 (NKJV)

Heaven is a spiritual world that functions under God's Government. He created the earth to function in reflection to how He functions in Heaven. God's will is being done in Heaven, but it can only be done here on Earth through cooperation with Man. Jesus teaches us to pray, "Thy Kingdom come, Thy will be done, on earth as it is in Heaven."[29] Prayer is Man's lifeline here on earth. It is the means by which we speak and communicate with God.

The more time you spend with God in prayer, the more your knowledge in Him will grow. This will help you pray more effectively. You can know God through His Word. As you become more familiar with the Holy Spirit during prayer, you will be able to pray to the will of God. Knowing God's will, thus, enables us to pray God's desires into any given situation.

The Bible is clear on the qualification that whatever is asked, it must be according to the will of God in faith. Jesus' public prayers were short, plain, and direct, but in private we see Him spending a great deal of time with the Father. Jesus said when we pray, we must go into our prayer closet. The purpose of all prayer is to give God honor and to pray His will.

> *"Father, if it is Your will take this cup away from Me nevertheless not My will, but Yours be done."*[30]

---

29 Matthew 6:10 (New American Standard Bible)
30 Luke 22:42 (NKJV)

Jesus prayed this prayer a few times before He was arrested. Our human nature can be very persuasive in convincing us to do things that we should not. It can be very difficult at times to obey what the Word of God says. The Apostle Paul said it this way, "I don't really understand myself, for I want to do what is right, but I don't do it. Instead, I do what I hate. But if I know that what I am doing is wrong, this shows that I agree that the law is good. So I am not the one doing wrong; it is sin living in me that does it. And I know that nothing good lives in me, that is, in my sinful nature. I want to do what is right, but I can't."[31]

Our human nature always seeks its own will, not the will of God. So, how do we get over this? I'm glad you asked. It's only by having a daily dose of the Word of God that you will overcome. Taking in even a scripture verse a day will do wonders for the spirit-man. Knowing what God's Word says makes it easy to pray the will of God. Our hearts must be pure before God so that we can be led by the Holy Spirit to honor Him in prayer.

"For as many as are led, by the Spirit of God, these are sons of God."[32]

Sometimes scripture may not give the answer to a situation that you are going through. At this point you need the Holy Spirit to guide you to make the right decision for that situation. Before Jesus went back to Heaven, He promised

---

31 Romans 7:15—18 (NLT)
32 Romans 8:14 (NKJV)

that He would send the Holy Spirit to be with us on Earth. The Bible calls Him the Comforter, who will guide you into all truth.

We give God glory when we come into agreement with His Word. Jesus' flesh cried out, so He prayed, "If it is possible, let this cup pass from Me."[33] But then He came into alignment with God's will and prayed, "Nevertheless, not as I will, but as You will."[34] Jesus needed to be strengthened at that moment. Every one of us has moments like that. Sometimes we know His will, but we find it hard to follow, and other times we struggle to know what His will is. Thank God that we have the Holy Spirit to help us through difficult times. When we are unable to understand God's will, the Holy Spirit will pray through us. If we study Bible scriptures, when we find ourselves unable to pray, the Holy Spirit will bring those scriptures back to our minds. The Holy Spirit also ministers to the believer and convicts our conscience when we are going the wrong way.

We are told in Ephesians to pray in the spirit on all occasions with all kinds of prayers and requests. With this in mind, be alert, and always keep praying for the saints in Christ.

Prayer is necessary because of God's original plan. In Genesis, God commanded that Man have authority over the earth and all the works of His hand when he said, "Let them have dominion." God will not violate this command that He established between Heaven and Earth. God is

---

33   Matthew 26:39 (NKJV)

34   Matthew 26:39 (NKJV)

a Spirit, so for Him to physically come to the earth, He became a man. In order for Him to accomplish anything here on Earth, He does so through Man. That being so, it is the responsibility of Man to invite God to Earth through prayer. God gave Man the mandate to pray. According to God's original law, only Man has the legal right to operate on Earth. However, because of Adam's sin and disobedience, Man lost that authority, allowing the enemy to operate freely. When Jesus died on the cross, that authority was given back to us. The grace we receive from Jesus, enables us to fulfill God's command.

Although we are told to pray, sometimes we can get disappointed and frustrated when our prayers are not answered. Unanswered prayers can be an obstacle to our faith. Becoming disappointed can cause someone to question God. You know the Word of God is supposed to work, so why is there no answer to your prayer, you may ask? When this happens, a believer may feel abandoned and isolated from God, and then come to the wrong conclusion about themselves and the Lord.

Sometimes prayers are not answered because there are hindrances (which we will discuss in chapter seven). Other times, prayers are answered but not the way we want. This is because God is sovereign and knows what's best for us. So He will sometimes give us what we need rather than what we asked for in prayer. However, there are times, God is just saying "wait." He hears our prayers. When we don't hear an answer, it does not mean that He is denying our request. God is faithful in answering prayer. Jesus asks us to pray because He knows our prayers will be answered. The response, though, is sometimes delayed because God is working behind the scenes. Prayer works with love, patience, faithfulness, and forbearance.

Daniel was praying for twenty-one days before he received his answer.[35] The scripture tells us that God answered Daniel's prayer the very first day that he prayed. However, a principality that ruled over Persia blocked Gabriel the angel from delivering the message to Daniel. Michael, the archangel, had to come and contend with that principality to release Gabriel. Sometimes we just have to be persistent and patient in order to receive the answer to our prayer. Just imagine if Daniel had given up on the twentieth day. Most of the time we cannot see God working behind the scenes, we just have to trust Him.

"Trust in the Lord with all your heart and lean not on your own understanding. In all your ways acknowledge Him, and He will direct your paths."[36]

Listen to what David said in Psalm 40:1–2 (NLT):

"I waited patiently for the Lord to help me, and He turned to me and heard my cry. He lifted me out of the pit of despair out of the mud and mire. He set my feet on solid ground and steadied me as I walked along."

---

35   Daniel 10:1–15 (KJV)
36   Proverbs 3:5—6 (KJV)

God wants us to grow in our faith; praying without understanding is ineffective. Building intimacy with God, and honoring His nature and character, will give you understanding of His will. If you find yourself stuck in any circumstance, know that while you're waiting, God is working it out. If God is for you, then, who can be against you? Have faith in God.

PRAISE BREAK
Psalm 109:30

I will greatly praise the Lord with my mouth. Yes, I will praise Him among the multitude. I give Him all the praise.

PRAYER
Father, let Your kingdom come, and let Your will be done in my life. You promised to supply all my needs according to your riches in glory, so I come into agreement with what You are doing in my life and my family. Open my eyes so that I can understand Your will for me in Your Word. I trust You, Lord. In Jesus' Name. Amen 🙏

TAKE AWAY
- We pray to make our requests and petitions known. Our requests must line up with God's Word and His will for our lives.

Chapter 4

Praying the Will of God in Your Circumstances (The Lord's Prayer)

IN THE GOSPELS, we see Jesus praying and talking to God at all times. He said, "My Father is always working, and so am I."[37] This can only happen when you are having continual conversations with the Father.

Prayer is the most common practice in all religions of the world, yet it is still the most misunderstood activity in our day. Prayer is Man exercising his God-given authority to ask for Heaven's influence to be on earth. God answers our prayers as soon as we ask, however, the answer manifests in His timing.

Take this book for example. God spoke to me in 2009 to start writing. Every time I made an attempt to label the book completed, the Holy Spirit impressed on me that

---

37   John 5:17 (NLT)

it was not the right timing. If I had published this book back then, you may not be reading what you are reading now. So, do not get discouraged if you have unanswered prayers. Delay is not always denial. Continue to pray and trust God's timing.

In Matthew 6:9–13, Jesus gave us a blueprint of how to pray. He said, "After this manner therefore pray ye…" This prayer doesn't have to be recited word for word, rather it is to guide you on how to approach God and what to ask of Him.

Jesus taught His disciples to pray in sincerity and simplicity. He also told them to add fasting and giving to their prayer life. He instructed them not to use vain repetitions but to enter into their closet and shut the door.[38] Jesus left us this pattern to follow in the Lord's Prayer." His opening words were "Our Abba" meaning "Our Father." Here is a breakdown of the Lord's Prayer.

"Our Father in Heaven…"[39] This prayer begins by establishing God's supreme authority and our relationship with Him. We recognize the greatness of where He lives; far above us. He is the Creator of the heavens and Earth, who knows the exact location of everything at every moment. As our Father, He is our source, sustainer, protector and defender.

"Hallowed be Your Name…"[40] Hallowed means sacred, consecrated, and entitled to reverence. Reverence means

---

[38] Matthew 6:6–7(NKJV)
[39] Matthew 6:9 (NKJV)
[40] ibid

honor or respect shown; profound respect, adoration, and awe. True reverence prevents us from carelessly approaching God. Properly recognizing God promotes sincerity, carefulness, honesty, and humility in prayer.

"Your Kingdom come…"[41] We welcome the Kingdom of God and desire to unite with Him and His will. We pray for wisdom to understand what scripture says about us and pray back the Word to Him.

"Your will be done, on earth as it is in Heaven…"[42] In this we confess that we want to fit into God's will instead of trying to fit Him into ours. We also pray that others will accept and do His will as well. The believer recognizes his weaknesses and humbles himself before God. Our Heavenly Father knew we would need help knowing what to pray for, so He gave us His Spirit to help us so that we could pray effectively.

> *"Likewise, the Spirit also helpeth our infirmities for we know not what we should pray for as we ought: but the Spirit Himself makes intercession for us with groans which cannot be uttered."*[43]

"Give us this day our daily bread…"[44] This request honors God as our provider. Christ reminds us that this should be our daily request. We show our trust in the Lord

---

41 Matthew 6:10 (NKJV)
42 ibid
43 Romans 8:26 (KJV)
44 Matthew 6:11 (NKJV)

when we ask for enough for today. The believer must have faith in the power, wisdom, and goodness of God. Jesus said, "Therefore I tell you, whatever you ask for in prayer, believe that you have received it, and it will be yours."[45]

"Forgive us our debts as we forgive our debtors…"[46] This petition cannot be divided. We cannot expect God to forgive us if we do not forgive those who have wronged us. We have a moral obligation to forgive those who have hurt us. When we come before God to pray, we must forgive others as well as ask for forgiveness in order to have access to Heaven.

> *"And whenever you stand praying, if you have anything against anyone, forgive him, that your Father in heaven may also forgive you your trespasses."*[47]

> *"The heart is deceitful above all things, and desperately wicked who can know it?"*[48]

Only God knows our heart, so to protect us He said to forgive when we pray.

"Do not lead us into temptation…"[49] Although we know that God will not lead us into temptation, by requesting this we correctly state God's will and remind ourselves that without His power, we will sin.

---

[45] Mark 11:24 (NIV)
[46] Matthew 6:12 (NKJV)
[47] Mark 11:25 (NKJV)
[48] Jeremiah 17:9 (NKJV)
[49] Matthew 6:13 (NKJV)

"Deliver us from the evil one…"[50] Here we express a desire not to be tempted to sin. This is asking God to deliver us from doing evil and from others who would do evil to us. We must examine our hearts so that we do not pray with the wrong motives. Our hearts can sometimes deceive us into believing that God is pleased with us, when in fact we are in sin.

"Yours is the Kingdom…"[51] This exalts God and acknowledges His rightful ownership and kingship over His Kingdom. At the same time, we admit that the Kingdom belongs to Him.

"The power…"[52] He is the King of kings and the Lord of lords, the Almighty. He has the power over everything.

> *"The earth is the Lord's and the fullness thereof the world and they that dwell therein."*[53]

When you are before Him in prayer, you must remember that everything belongs to the Lord.

"The glory…"[54] All glory rightfully belongs to God, and He will share it with no other.

---

50 ibid
51 ibid
52 ibid
53 Psalm 24:1 (KJV)
54 ibid

> *"You have taught the little children to praise you perfectly. May their example shame and silence your enemies!"*[55]

Give God praise and glory for who He is, and not only for the things he has done. Praising the Lord will keep your mind in peace so the enemy will not be able to discourage you.

> *"Know ye that the Lord He is God it is He that hath made us, and not we ourselves, we are His people and the sheep of His pasture."*[56]

Know that whatever we accomplish, God gets all the glory. This keeps us humble in prayer.

"Forever…"[57] Our God is eternal. He does not change. He will always exist with the highest authority, the strongest power, and the greatest glory.

"Amen."[58] So let it be.

---

55 Psalm 8:2 (TLB)
56 Psalm 100:3 (KJV)
57 Matthew 6:13 (NKJV)
58 ibid

PRAISE BREAK
Psalm 150:6

All the praise, all the glory, and all the honor belongs to you, Lord. I praise You with everything within me.

PRAYER
Abba Father, I come to You knowing that You are a good Father. Thank You for forgiving me of my sins. Help me to forgive those who hurt me. I ask for strength for today to accomplish all that I need to get done. Guide me through the decisions I need to make this day. Teach me to love and have patience. In Jesus Christ's Name. Amen. 🙏

TAKE AWAY
- Before requesting anything from God, give Him reverence.
- Whatever you are requesting from God should be according to His will, and not according to your desire.

Chapter 5

We Pray for Growth and Transformation

GROWING FAITH TRANSFORMS a believer's life. Prayer is the hand that holds the key. The key is the faith that opens the door.

> *"The just shall live by his faith..."*[59]

Faith should be a lifestyle for Christians. We need to meditate on God's Word continually so that it gets into our hearts, and we can live our daily lives trusting Him. Faith is a spiritual power that grows and develops in the soul of Man. It is not isolated; it works with love and patience.

The counsel of God works to develop a strong spiritual person. We must obey the principles of God so that when we speak His Word, it will manifest in our lives. The

---

59 Habakkuk 2:4 (NKJV)

more you remember biblical and personal ways that God answers prayer, the stronger the foundation of your confidence in prayer will become.

You must have faith in the One you are praying to. The believer should pray whatever honors God to advance His Kingdom. When we trust and submit to God, the Holy Spirit helps us to pray with understanding, which unleashes Heaven's power in our lives. Jesus said, "The words that I speak unto you are spirit, and they are life."[60]

> *"Death and life are in the power of the tongue, and those who love it will eat its fruit."*[61]

Words are spirit, and so they have the ability to produce life in your circumstances. When the answers to your petitions do not manifest immediately, you must exercise patience and stand on the promises of God. When you have done all the things you are called to do—prayed, fasted, and given to the poor—keep standing on the Word of God, and your faith will become perfect and strong.

Patience strengthens your faith. It takes perseverance sometimes to wait on God, but your confidence should always be in Him. When the Word of God is planted in the heart, faith will grow. Believe and confess what the Bible says, not what you are feeling or thinking. Faith is not a mental exercise. It is not logical. You will not be able to understand it, so you just have to believe it, and then act

---

60   John 6:63 (NKJV)
61   Proverbs 18:21 (NKJV)

on it. We are told to request things from God in the right way because we can ask amiss.

> *"And even when you do ask you don't get it because your whole aim is wrong and you want only what will give you pleasure."*[62]

When we meditate on the Word of God, we will ask according to His will. There is nothing wrong with material things in their proper perspective, but when that is all we focus on, we will ask amiss.

> *"Listen to me, you can pray for anything and if you believe you have it, it is yours."*[63]

This means we must pray according to the will of God and His prompting in our hearts. When we pray like that, we are aligning our will to the Father's will. We can have desires for our loved ones to receive salvation, but we must ask the Holy Spirit to lead us when we are praying for them. Whatever things we desire, it should come into agreement with God's Word.

We can desire something for someone else, but we cannot force them to desire it too. God didn't put us in charge of other people's faith. We can pray for others, but we can't let our will transfer onto them to make them do what we want

---

[62] James 4:3 (TLB)
[63] Mark 11:24 (TLB)

them to do; that would be witchcraft. To make someone do what we want is to take away their free will.

> *"But without faith it is impossible to please Him for he that cometh to God must believe that He is, and that He is a rewarder of them that diligently seek Him."[64]*

Anyone that comes to God must believe that He is who He said He is. Total trust is required. You can have strong faith and still experience feelings that can cause you to make wrong decisions. Faith is the password; the key to receiving anything from God. Faith is not denying what is happening around you. You must recognize the facts as you see them, and then apply the truth of God's Word to your situation to get results. Continue to confess the Word of God in your particular circumstance, and see the glory of God manifest in your life.

> *"We can make our plans, but the final outcome is in God's hands."[65]*

Planning does not hinder your faith. God wants us to be diligent in every area of our life. He gave us emotions and feelings, but they were never meant to govern us. They are beneficial, but they should not be relied upon. When sorrow, despair, or depression comes, this should alert you

---
64 Hebrews 11:6 (NKJV)
65 Proverbs 16:1 (TLB)

to look to the Word of God for strength. When everything seems to be going wrong, do not look inside of yourself to your emotions and feelings. Your faith is being tested. Turn to God's Word.

The Bible should determine what we believe, not our feelings. When you are in faith, the Word of God governs you.

> *"What is faith? It is the confident assurance that something we want is going to happen. It is the certainty that what we hope for is waiting for us, even though we cannot see it up ahead."*[66]

Faith is the firm assurance that God will do whatever He promised to do. It is the conviction that God knows what He is doing even when you do not. Faith must be proved, which is only done when it is put to the test.

Abraham was determined to obey God regardless of the cost or consequence.[67] What was Abraham holding on to? He had the promise of God, the words He had told him; that he would be the father of many nations. If you come into great need by following God's command, the Lord will see to it that you lose nothing by your obedience.

Abraham did not know how his story was going to end. He confidently believed God, trusting that He would provide what was needed. Isaac said to his father, "Behold the fire and the wood, but where is the lamb for a burnt

---

66 Hebrews 11:1 (TLB)
67 Genesis 22:1—19 (NKJV)

offering?" Abraham answered with confidence, "Have faith in God. God will provide."[68]

This is the same way that God provides for His children today. His provision for us in Christ through His death at Calvary has given us the guarantee that all our necessities, both carnal and spiritual, are provided by Him. The Apostle Paul said, "He that spared not His own Son but delivered Him up for us all, how shall He not with Him freely give us all things?"[69]

Wow! Hallelujah! Glory to God! The Lord will give us all things promised in the covenant, when we trust Him. Have you ever found yourself thinking, "People who do not know God are having a good time, so why am I having such a hard time?" Well, you are in good company.

Read Psalm 73 in its entirety. The psalmist writes in verses twelve and thirteen, "Behold these are the ungodly, who prosper in the world, they increase in riches. Verily I have cleansed my heart in vain and washed my hands in innocence." Sometimes we can get into a debate with God, asking why things are the way they are. What do you do when God does the opposite of what you've asked of Him? Do you sometimes try to tell God what to do, and how He should do it? You are not alone.

The psalmist came to a conclusion in verses 18–26. Verse twenty-six says, "My flesh and my heart failed, but God is the strength of my heart, and my portion forever." God

---

[68] Genesis 22:7—8 (NKJV)
[69] Romans 8:32 (KJV)

will never leave you alone. He will always be by your side, even when you can't understand the situation you are in.

This reminds me of Habakkuk, who complained to God about his situation, as it appeared to him that others were getting away with wrong-doing. After God gave Habakkuk the revelation of what He was about to do to Babylon, Habakkuk was reassured, and he gave God praise.

> *"Even though the fig trees are all destroyed and there is neither blossom left nor fruit; though the olive crops all fail, and the fields lie barren; even if the flocks die in the fields and the cattle barns are empty, yet I will rejoice in the Lord I will be happy in the God of my salvation. The Lord God is my strength he will give me the speed of a deer and bring me safely over the mountains."[70]*

The Apostle Paul also experienced problems in life. He was in a situation where he asked God three times to take away the thorn in his flesh.[71] The Corinthian church was under attack from people with wrong motives. They were speaking against Paul's first letter to the church, saying he was bold in his writing but the worst preacher in person. This put Paul in a position where he had to defend himself. He did not like doing it, but he had to. Paul had to prove that he was not just coming by his own authority, but he was called by God.

---

70 Habakkuk 3:17–19 (TLB)
71 2 Corinthians 12:7–11 (KJV)

Paul shared with them his deep love and affection for them, and his fear that they would be led away and deceived by Satan, as Eve was in the Garden of Eden. Paul had to expose the motives of false teachers that were in the church. In doing so he had to be harsh. He had to testify of the things he had gone through.

Paul had four encounters with the risen Christ, and these gave him great revelations. He said, "And lest I should be exalted above measure through the abundance of the revelations there was given to me a thorn in the flesh, the messenger of Satan to buffet me, lest I should be exalted above measure."[72] Paul prayed three times. He asked, then went back a second and a third time to ask again. God's answer was, "My grace is sufficient for you, for my strength is made perfect in weakness."[73]

God did not remove Paul's problem. He said His grace was sufficient, and He used suffering to display His grace. God uses suffering to project His power in us, to draw us to Him, and to humble us. Sometimes there has to be some sifting in order to get to the root of any problem of the heart. Without the suffering, how will you know if you truly have faith in God? He knows your heart. He lets you go through situations so that you can see what is in your heart. God doesn't always remove the problem, but He gives you the power to go through the stress of it. He gives you what you need to succeed in every trial.

---

72 2 Corinthians 12:7 (KJV)
73 2 Corinthians 12:9 (KJV)

PRAISE BREAK
Psalm 103:1

Bless the Lord, oh my soul, and all that is within me, bless His holy name. I give you all my worship.

PRAYER
Father, I pray to be filled with the knowledge of Your will, and that in all wisdom and spiritual understanding I will be able to walk worthy of Your will and be pleasing in your sight. Let me be filled with Your love so that my life will be pleasing to you. In Jesus Christ's Name. Amen 🙏

TAKE AWAY
- We pray for growth and transformation. Growing faith transforms a believer's life. Prayer is the hand that holds the key. The key is the faith that opens the door.

Chapter 6

We Do Warfare in Prayer

WHILE IN WARFARE, we must know how to fight defensively and offensively. All prayer is declaring war in the spiritual kingdom. You are taking a side. There are two kingdoms that are contending for your attention. The war started in Heaven. We do not have the resources or power to win in this warfare by ourselves. We need to know what the Word of God says about the enemy. Knowing the enemy will give us the insight on how to be victorious.

We are human, but we don't engage in this fight with human weapons, for the weapons of our warfare are not with the flesh, they are spiritual.[74] These spiritual weapons are powerful enough to destroy massive fortresses. We fight with weapons that the Holy Spirit inspires in us, destroying speculations and every deceitful lie that is raised up

---
74   2 Corinthians 10:3–5 (The Amplified Bible)

against the Word of truth. Speculations, ideas, theories, viewpoints, and lies that come against the knowledge of God. You must bring every thought captive to the obedience of Christ.

> *"Finally, my brethren, be strong in the Lord and in the power of His might. Put on the whole armor of God, that ye may be able to stand against the wiles of the devil. For we wrestle not against flesh and blood, but against principalities, against powers, against the rulers of the darkness of this world, against spiritual wickedness in high places. Wherefore take unto you the whole armor of God, that ye may be able to withstand in the evil day, and having done all to stand. Stand therefore having your loins girt about with truth, and having on the breastplate of righteousness, and your feet shod with the preparation of the gospel of peace. Above all taking the shield of faith, wherewith ye shall be able to quench all the fiery darts of the wicked. And take the helmet of salvation and the sword of the Spirit, which is the word of God. Praying always with all prayer and supplication in the Spirit, and watching thereunto with all perseverance and supplication for all saints."*[75]

We are told to put on the armor of God:

---

[75] Ephesians 6:10–18 (KJV)

The Belt of Truth. You must be committed to being disciplined in the Word of God to know what the scriptures say. Having a relationship with Christ will allow the Holy Spirit to help you understand the truth of the Bible. Without knowing the truth, the other pieces of armor can be penetrated by the evil one. It is the very person and nature of God that defines truth. Truth is a person. He is Jesus Christ.

> *"Jesus said to him, 'I am the way and the truth and the life. No one comes to the Father except through Me.'"*[76]

> *"And you shall know the truth and the truth shall make you free."*[77]

Jesus loved you and valued you enough to die for you. Having a relationship with Him gives you peace of mind, a clear conscience, and healthy self-esteem. Jesus is the Truth.

The Breastplate of Righteousness. We receive Jesus' righteousness when we receive Him as Lord in our lives. Personal holiness is also important to win the battle. A pattern of sin makes you vulnerable to the evil one. Your relationship with God and Man is important to be in right standing.

---

76 John 14:6 (NJKV)
77 John 8:32 (NKJV)

Feet Shod with the Preparation of the Gospel of Peace. The peace of God holds you while in the middle of the battle. God is your defender and protector. This should give you peace of mind. It should make you fight with confidence, knowing that the Lord is with you. You carry the peace of God wherever you go. As you share the good news of peace, the Word of God empowers you to move forward and share the gospel with readiness. The believer must be equipped and prepared on the inside with the Word of God.

> *"Be diligent to present yourself approved to God, a worker who does not need to be ashamed, rightly dividing the word of truth."*[78]

The Shield of Faith. With your shield of faith, you quench the temptations that Satan sends your way. The devil comes with deceptive lies that can lure you into sin. Believing in the Word of God will shield you from the lies. It is your faith in God's Word that protects you from believing a lie. This is a full-body length shield that will protect every aspect of the believer's life. Their faith in God will quench, extinguish, and put out the fiery darts. A person must believe not only that the true God exists, but that He will also fulfill His promise to reward Man's faith in Him with forgiveness and righteousness.

---

[78] 2 Timothy 2:15 (NKJV)

> *"But without faith it is impossible to please Him for he who comes to God must believe that He is and that He is a rewarder of those who diligently seek Him."*[79]

The Helmet of Salvation. Satan preys on you in times of weakness. Knowing that you have salvation secures you in Christ. The helmet of salvation protects that knowledge. Know that all your sins have been forgiven and that you have a future with God. You are a one-of-a-kind original person, created in God's image and likeness, and designed to relate to Him. Know that you are a seed of Abraham through Jesus Christ. It is important to know who you are in Christ so that you do not just follow your feelings, which change from day to day whereas God's love never changes. You must know that you have been given the free gift of salvation through Jesus' dying on the cross and protect that knowledge at all costs.

> *"Just as He chose us in Him before the foundation of the world, that we should be holy and without blame before Him in love."* [80]

> *"Therefore, if anyone is in Christ, he is a new creation, old things have passed away; behold all things have become new."*[81]

---

[79] Hebrews 11:6 (NKJV)
[80] Ephesians 1:4 (NKJV)
[81] 2 Corinthians 5:17 (NKJV)

The Sword of the Spirit. This is the Word of God. Having a physical Bible doesn't help when you are in a battle. You must have the Word in your heart so that you can speak it out in times of spiritual warfare. The Word of God is sufficient for our salvation. It is able to convert a soul and make the simple or ignorant person wise and fully skilled in all matters of holy living. God's Word is infallible, inerrant, complete, and authoritative. It is sufficient to accomplish all of God's will and purposes for your life and in your life. The Word of God is the source of all truth, and it brings people to the knowledge of the truth.

> *"For the word of God is quick and powerful, and sharper than any two-edged sword piercing even to the division of soul and spirit and of joints and marrow and is a discerner of the thoughts and intents of the heart."*[82]

Remember, we are told to put on every piece of this armor. It will take great effort to do this. Even though we are sitting in a heavenly place in Christ, we are still in a wrestling tournament. This has nothing to do with another human being, but rather with spirits from another realm.

The weapons that we need for battle come from God's Word, and not from what we think or feel. These weapons only work when we demonstrate the lifestyle of the One who died for our sins (Jesus). These weapons are most powerful when spoken out of our mouths in prayer or while

---

82   Hebrews 4:12 (KJV)

making positive declarations or affirmations about our lives and following through with corresponding actions.

In Ephesians[83], Paul reminds the people that their strength must come from the Lord's power that is within them. They are to put on the armor of God so that they will be able to stand against all the strategies and tricks of Satan. You cannot walk in the newness of life with an old mindset. To experience the fullness of the blessings of God, you must be obedient to His Word. It can't be done in your own strength. We have an enemy who is going to do everything in his power to prevent us from living the way God wants us to live. Satan hates God and all those who are in His kingdom. We are up against a supernatural system that comes through the sinful tendencies of our human nature. Satan is the prince of this world, and he works through the world system. To resist evil and stand, you need to put on the full armor of God.

We show others the truth of the Word of God, and we also defend ourselves with His Word. Your defense is not just the truth, but knowing the truth. The Word of God has to be used with the right precision. If you are ignorant of any area of biblical truth, then you will be defenseless in that area of your life. It is the specific use of scripture, followed by divine principles applied to your life, that will bring you victory.

Jesus while on earth lived a life that we can follow. He is waiting for you to ask Him for help in your prayer life. Jesus taught His disciples to pray in sincerity, humility,

---

83 Ephesians 6:10—11 (NKJV)

and simplicity. He said, "When you pray, enter into your closet and shut the door."[84] Jesus taught His disciples to add fasting to their prayer, telling them, "When you fast, anoint your head."[85] That means you don't have to look like you are fasting. Jesus's disciples asked Him how to pray. Of all the great things Jesus did, they asked Him to teach them how to pray. Praying in the Spirit will build your spirit. Spend time listening to God before you begin to pray. In this way you will be praying in the will of God. You will never get to a point where you will need to stop praying. Praying the will of God will change you from the inside out, and this process takes a lifetime.

---

84 Matthew 6:6 (KJV)
85 Matthew 6:17 (KJV)

PRAISE BREAK
Psalm 136:1

Oh, give thanks unto the Lord, for He is good, and His mercy endures forever. I will praise Him in the morning, at noon time, and the evening.

PRAYER
Thank you, Lord, for I am established in Your righteousness, and oppression is far from me. I am blessed with all spiritual blessings in the heavenly places in Christ Jesus. According to Your Word no weapon that forms against me shall prosper in my life, and every tongue that rises against me in judgment I condemn it, for this is my heritage. I put on the armor of God and stand against every lie of the enemy. In Jesus Christ's Name. Amen 🙏

TAKE AWAY
- We do warfare in prayer. We need to know the enemy through the Word of God. The enemy is not human but spirits without bodies.

Chapter 7

Hindrances to Prayer

SOMETIMES WHEN YOU have prayed for a while and do not get any reply, it may seem like Heaven is brass, meaning that it feels like you are engaging in one-way communication. You want answers, but there are none to your requests. There is no light shining through your prayer. You have used up all the words in your vocabulary, and you do not know what else to do. At this point some Christians give up and stop praying. This breakdown in communication could be because you, as a mature believer, are in spiritual warfare with Satan, causing God to deliberately not attend to your prayer in that moment.

There are three things that can break down the flow of communication from Heaven to Earth.

1. God is pruning you. He wants more fruit from your life, but you are resisting.

2. Unconfessed sin. You are not right with God.
3. Broken relationships. You are not right with others.

Pruning is about growth. Sometimes Christians have a hard time distinguishing between discipline and pruning in their walk with God. The reason for pruning is to remove dead or dying things around the believer. God wants the believer to grow in their prayer life; seeking and trusting Him more. He wants to bring the believer to a place of revelation so that their understanding can be enlightened. The Father wants to increase the quality of the believer's ministry, developing and maturing them to a higher level. Without pruning, the believer will only live up to a fraction of their potential.

Sometimes God allows trials to happen to Christians in order to bring self-sufficiency to an end. Self-sufficiency is when the believer thinks they can fulfill the purpose of God on their own. He purposely takes them out of their comfort zone and brings them face to face with storms and trials. A believer must learn obedience and allow God's will to be done. Jesus said, "If any man will come after me let him deny himself, and take up his cross daily, and follow me."[86] Moses had to confront Pharaoh, Jacob had to wrestle with the Angel of the Lord, Joseph had to become a slave, and Jesus had to die on the cross to bring about the will of God.

If you are going to follow in Jesus' footsteps, you will have to remove all the idols and restrictions in your life.

---
86 Luke 9:23 (KJV)

When a believer is being broken by God and bitterness and unforgiveness is in their heart, God will not attend to that believer's prayer. If your relationship with God is injured, apologize today for your attitude and thoughts, and then move on.

> *"My brethren count it all joy when you fall into various trials, knowing that the testing of your faith produces patience. But let patience have its perfect work, that you may be perfect and complete, lacking nothing."*[87]

You are not right with God. Your actions towards God may not be pleasing to Him. Perhaps you are sinning against Him in your actions or attitudes. Disobedience to God's commandments can be a hindrance in your prayer life.

> *"And whatsoever we ask, we receive from Him, because we keep His commandments, and do those things that are pleasing in His sight."*[88]

You may be sinning against the Lord in your attitude and not realize it. Your attitude could be like Job's, telling God what to do when He is putting you through a test. Are you bitter towards Him because of a situation you are in? Christians can sometimes feel like God has abandoned

---

87 James 1:2–4 (NKJV)
88 1 John 3:22 (NKJV)

them, causing anger to seep into their hearts. Remember to ask the Holy Spirit to look into your heart and reveal any hidden sin. The Holy Spirit speaks to your conscience, but if you are ignoring His voice, He may become silent.

> "Quench not the Spirit."[89]

> *"Don't cause the Holy Spirit sorrow by the way you live. Remember He is the one who marks you to be present on that day when salvation from sin will be complete."*[90]

You are not right with others: When breakdown happens with family members or friends it can hit hard in the heart and leave scars. Forgiveness is necessary for prayers to be answered. This is why daily prayer is needed so that the Holy Spirit can let you know when you are holding on to unforgiveness.

Evil spirits are everywhere, waiting for you to stay in your sin so they can tempt you into an even deeper sin of unforgiveness. Forgive quickly so that you can begin the healing process. Unforgiveness can lead to bitterness taking root. Bitterness then leads to resentment, which leads to hatred. Yes, what was done to you was not fair, but how you react to it is also important to the Lord Jesus.

---

89   1 Thessalonians 5:19 (KJV)
90   Ephesians 4:30 (TLB)

Let us consider the story of Absalom in 2 Samuel 13. I will give you the short version. (Please read 2 Samuel for the full account.)

King David loved his son Absalom. He wanted him to become the next king. Absalom had a sister named Tamar. The Bible says she was fair, which means she was beautiful. Amnon, their half-brother who was from a different mother, was in love with Tamar, his half-sister. He lied to get Tamar alone with him and raped her. When he finished having his fun, he told his servant to put her out of his house. This was a disgraceful thing to happen to a princess. The news reached King David. The Bible says David was very wroth, but he did not give justice to Tamar. Just think about this story and how Tamar must have felt.

Without saying a word to his half-brother, Absalom took his sister into his house and took care of her. He waited for some time to pass for his father to do something, but nothing happened. Absalom took matters into his own hands, which ended in Amnon's death. Absalom later lost his life by trying to take his father's throne by force.

It was unfair what Amnon did to his half-sister. She was once a royal virgin held in high esteem. It was unjust that it was by the king's command that she went to serve her brother. Tamar's life as she knew it was over. She was now robed in shame, while the man who committed this sin was living like nothing had happened.

Our hearts are like soil. The seed is the Word of God. When the Word of God takes root in our hearts it will produce the fruit of righteousness. The soil will only produce what is planted in it. Absalom's thoughts were poisoned with bitterness, he refused to forgive, and he became an enemy of Amnon, his brother and David, his father.

There are some people who are offended who were truly treated unjustly, and there are some people who are offended who merely believe they were treated unjustly. The outcome of being offended in either scenario is the same. If you do not deal with an offense it will produce more fruit of sin. Those who believe they have been treated unjustly get their conclusion from inaccurate information, or their information is accurate, but their conclusion is distorted.

This is a trap from the enemy. It works well because we think we have a right to have anger towards the offender. The enemy of our souls is subtle and delights on deception. You may think you are over an offense, but then something similar happens and all the pain comes back.

If you are experiencing pain, please don't stop reading. You have to get to the root of the offenses. This can take time because of the magnitude of the pain that was caused by the offender. You may need time away from this person in order to heal. You are not alone. Jesus is always there to help us through. He understands because He went through the pain of others unjustly hurting Him.

Jesus said when we pray, we must forgive, and then our Heavenly Father will forgive us. Offended people produce fruits of jealousy, strife, anger, envy, bitterness, outrage, resentment, and hatred. One way the enemy keeps a person in an offended state is to keep the offense hidden and cloaked with pride. Pride will keep you from admitting your true condition, and it will cause you to view yourself as a victim. Your heart condition may be hidden from you, but it is not hidden from God. When you have been mistreated and you hold the pain in your heart, it takes a longer time for healing to take place. Letting go is not easy, but it is the beginning of the healing process.

Read Genesis 45:5–8. Through all of Joseph's circumstances in life, he remained pliable to God's processes in preparing him for His purpose. God has a purpose for every believer. He is in control of our destiny. No one else. It is more important to submit to God's way than to be proven right. Do not be afraid to allow the Holy Spirit to reveal any unforgiveness or bitterness in your heart. We must examine our hearts and open ourselves to correction from the Lord. Only the Word of God is able to discern the thoughts and intentions of the heart.

> *"For the word of God is living and powerful and sharper than any two-edged sword, piercing even to the division of soul and spirit, and of joints and marrow, and is a discerner of the thoughts and intents of the heart."*[91]

Deception can make you believe with all your heart that you are right about something, when in reality, you are wrong. A person who refuses to obey the Word of God deceives his own heart. Harboring an offense gives a false

---

91   Hebrews 4:12 (NKJV)

sense of self-protection. It keeps you from seeing your own character flaws because you blame someone else for your pain. If you have been hurt, please don't stop praying. Get to the root of the wrong-doing so you can forgive. Forgiving others frees you from bitterness.

At times God will use a person's hurt to minister to others. God refines us with offenses and trials. When we go through these tribulations it reveals what is in our hearts. It puts our character on display. When you walk in a selfish love, expecting others to meet your expectations, you can easily become disappointed, hurt, and offended. Yet be encouraged that when we are going through that pain, God is there to help us if we allow Him. The first step, however, is forgiveness. It is only by forgiving that we are able to receive peace. It isn't always easy to let go and forgive, but it is the best path forward in the process of healing your heart. Guard your heart from offense.

PRAISE BREAK
Psalm 51:1

Have mercy upon me, O Lord, according to Your love and kindness, and according to the multitude of Your tender mercy. Thank you for Your mercy.

PRAYER
Father, forgive me for sinning against You. I repent of the sin in my thoughts, deeds, and actions. Create in me a clean heart. Take away all guilt and shame. Let the words of my mouth and the meditation of my heart be acceptable in Your sight, my Lord and my Redeemer. In Jesus Christ's Name. Amen 🙏

TAKE AWAY
- God will not hear us when we are resisting Him, when we have unconfessed sin, and when we hold unforgiveness in our hearts. These things hinder our prayers.

Chapter 8

The Power of Thought

MAN HAS THREE parts that make him a total being. The **body,** the **spirit,** and the **soul.** When we understand these three parts it becomes easier to live a victorious life in God. Man lives in a body, has a spirit, and makes decisions with the soul.

> *"Now may the God of peace Himself sanctify you completely; and may your whole spirit, soul, and body be preserved blameless at the coming of our Lord Jesus Christ."*[92]

The body is the outer part of Man that you can see with your eyes. The windows of the body are the five senses: seeing, hearing, tasting, smelling, and feeling. Through the

---

[92] 1 Thessalonians 5:23 (NKJV)

five senses information goes to the soul, good or bad. We are influenced by what we see, hear, taste, smell, and feel. Man spends a great deal of money taking care of the body. Our body is God's temple, and we are to keep it holy.[93] When you think of what He has done for us, is this too much to ask?

> *"And so dear brothers I plead with you to give your bodies to God. Let them be a living sacrifice, holy the kind He can accept."*[94]

The body will change to dust when it dies, but the soul and spirit of Man will live forever, with God or separated from Him.

The spirit is the essence of Man, considered divine in origin. Adam became a living being only when God breathed into his nostrils.[95] When God speaks to Man through His Word, the impression is on the spirit. Spirit to spirit. Jesus said, "God is a Spirit, and they that worship Him must worship Him in spirit and in truth."[96]

The soul is the primary life force of the body, or the inner part of Man. The soul was born and shaped in sin. We inherited this sinful nature from Adam. No one teaches a baby how to lie or steal. It comes to him or her naturally. Sin is the inherent nature of Man. The soul is the part of us

---

[93] 1 Corinthians 3:16 (NKJV)
[94] Romans 12:1 (TLB)
[95] Genesis 2:7 (NKJV)
[96] John 4:24 (NKJV)

that is the free moral agent. It experiences hunger, thirst, needs, and suffering. The soul has carnal needs, and it suffers when the body experiences trauma and when it is assaulted by passions of the flesh.

The soul is made up of three parts: mind, emotions, and will. Thoughts are in the mind, desires are the emotions, and choices are the will. When these three things connect, conception takes place.

In this chapter, in order to understand the power of thought, we will focus on the soul, wherein the mind is contained.

We are told to have the mind of Christ.[97] To achieve this, the soul has to be born again. Jesus said, "For a man to enter into the kingdom of God he must be born again."[98] To be born again is to be born of the Spirit of God. This is when we accept Jesus Christ as our Lord and Savior.

Even if you have been born again, God still asks you to come to Him through prayer. Your life will be a reflection of your mindset, and your mindset is developed through prayer. It is your mind that will lead you into tomorrow. Your mentality has the capacity to grow and to change. The Word of God is the only agent that can transform your mind.

> *"Don't copy the behavior and customs of this world, but be a new and different person with a fresh newness in all you do and think.*

---

[97] Philippians 2:5 (KJV)
[98] John 3:3 (KJV)

> *Then you will learn from your own experience how His ways will really satisfy you."*[99]

> *"And do not be conformed to this world, but be transformed by the renewing of your mind that you may prove what is that good and acceptable and perfect will of God."*[100]

Conforming refers to our outward expression. In the verse above, the Apostle Paul tells us not to conform to this world's systems and beliefs. The believer must transform by changing the attitude, demeanor, ways, direction, conduct, and ambitions that he or she had before salvation. The believer's outward expression should come from the regenerated inner man.

To renew your mind, you must make the decision to walk by faith and be objective about what thoughts you allow in. Man's mind is a battlefield. Satan attacks the mind with ideas that go against the Word of God. He has this world system under his control. The believer's mind is the point of attack. The battle is fought and won in the mind.

> *"Do not love the world or the things in the world. If anyone loves the world, the love of the Father is not in him. For all that is in the world - the lust*

---

99   Romans 12:2 (TLB)
100 Romans 12:2 (NKJV)

of the flesh, the lust of the eyes, and the pride of life - is not of the Father but is of the world."[101]

Satan cannot make you do anything against your will and, therefore, he bombards your mind so that you will be tempted to sin.

"Let no man say when he is tempted, I am tempted by God, for God cannot be tempted by evil nor does He Himself tempt anyone. But each one is tempted when he is drawn away by his own desires."[102]

"Therefore, submit to God, resist the devil, and he will flee from you."[103]

"The mind governed by the flesh is hostile to God; it does not submit to God's law, nor can it do so."[104]

Our minds resist God's law because of our sinful nature. With the help of the Holy Spirit, we can reprogram the mind. The Holy Spirit must regenerate and change the mind of the believer so that they will obey the Word of God. God's Spirit communicates with Man's spirit. Man's spirit then passes the information to the soul, where the mind is located. The mind then makes righteous decisions.

---

101 1 John 2:15–16 (NKJV)
102 James 1:13–14 (NKJV)
103 James 4:7 (NKJV)
104 Romans 8:7 (NIV)

Choices are made in the soul. You make decisions, actions follow, and your life tells the story of how you think.

You must get your thought-life aligned with what God's Word says. It is our responsibility to learn the ways of God. It will take more than just, "Good morning, Jesus," "Help me, Jesus," "Meet my needs, Jesus," and "Good night, Jesus." You will have to take the time to have a relationship with God.

> *"For the weapons of our warfare are not carnal but mighty in casting down arguments and every high thing that exalts itself against the knowledge of God, bringing every thought into captivity to the obedience of Christ."*[105]

> *"I use God's mighty weapons, not those made by men, to knock down the devil's strongholds. These weapons can break down every proud argument against God and every wall that can be built to keep men from finding Him. With these weapons I can capture rebels and bring them back to God and change them into men whose hearts' desire is obedience to Christ."*[106]

Christians have the mind of Christ in their spirit when they are consuming a daily dose of the scriptures. The mind will process the information given to it and come

---

[105] 2 Corinthians 10:4–5 (NKJV)
[106] 2 Corinthians 10:4–5 (TLB)

to conclusions based on what was put into it. This is called programming.

The kingdom of this world has the ability to program the natural mind or the carnal mind with its ungodly system. When your mind is renewed by the Word of God, it has the ability to transform from the natural or the carnal. We are called to focus consciously on our own thought patterns, and to continually ask ourselves whether our thoughts are glorifying God or serving ourselves.

The natural mind is the enemy of God. It is not subject to God's law or His ways. Man's spirit longs to move in the things of God, but the mind objects. The mind is programmed primarily by our five senses. Revelation of the Word is not easily received because the senses sometimes counteract it. The Holy Spirit has to be allowed to reprogram the mind from false beliefs. These are called strongholds. The enemy will try to overtake your mind. Satan knows that if your thinking is off-balance, he will have an opportunity to build a stronghold in your mind.

A stronghold is a belief in the mind where darkness reigns. It is a system of thinking rooted in a lie that a person has come to believe is the truth. A stronghold is any thought pattern different from the Word of God. It serves as a mental or emotional command centre to which the enemy has access. These thoughts are designed to mislead you into making wrong decisions using lies that appear as truths. We overcome strongholds when we make God's Word the filter of our thoughts. The strongholds are cleverly devised and patterned to make us believe that lies are actually the truth. Those nagging thoughts, suspicions, reasonings, and doubts are formed in a way to deceive us. Over time, if that person doesn't stop these thoughts, they will begin to believe that the thoughts are theirs.

We must believe what the Bible says. Only God's Word has the ability to pull down strongholds and fortresses. The wrong program in the mind, left alone for a long time, can attract evil spirits. Evil spirits can influence the mind and control the imagination. When this is the case, deliverance is required to set you free. These evil spirits can attach themselves to a thought or a concept that is rooted in a lie and build a stronghold in the mind. The demonic spirits then close the mind to the truth in order to strengthen the lie. This is why when a person makes the decision to do what is obviously wrong, it is very difficult to change that person's mind into doing what is right.

When thoughts and emotions meet, it starts a creative process. For example, if you hear a loud sound at night, you may experience the emotion of fear. Based on that emotion your thought may be that an intruder has entered your home. As a reaction of that thought your action may be to hide under your bed. Now, if that sound was merely the wind, then your thought that it was an intruder was wrong, rooted in fear, and your action was unnecessary or unfruitful. Emotions can lead to wrong thoughts, which can lead to inappropriate actions. Therefore, you must control your emotions and your thought patterns.

Evil spirits feed on wrong imaginations, random thoughts, impure desires, and unclean pictures. If you are unable to turn off evil thoughts, it is an evil spirit that is involved. You need deliverance immediately.

> *"These evil thoughts lead to evil actions and afterwards to the death penalty from God."*[107]

To become free from evil influence, you must spend time in God's presence in worship. Learn what His Word says about you. Walk in humility. Obey God's commands. Prayer in conjunction with fasting is also important. If you are intentional about your deliverance, you will experience freedom from bondage from the enemy. We are living in an evil world. Jesus said, "From the days of John the Baptist until now, the Kingdom of Heaven has suffered violence and men of violence take it by force."[108]

When interceding for others in prayer, the believer should keep his mind on the Word of God. As you intercede for a person, God will place on your heart what to pray for. It is wise to keep your heart in right standing with the Lord. No one is without sin, but there should not be habitual sin in your life. When you are interceding for others, you are coming against the kingdom of darkness, so you must be prepared for attacks from the enemy, ready with the Word of God.

As you fast and pray for others, the Lord will open your understanding. Remember that whatever revelations you receive, they must line up with the Word of God. If you

---

107 James 1:15 (TLB)
108 Matthew 11:12 (Revised Standard Version)

have a gift of prophecy, you will also get information from the kingdom of darkness. You must discern where the information is coming from.

Praying for others is us participating with God to establish the finished work of Christ and what He did on the cross. There are certain kinds of evil spirits which sit over a person and continually lie about others. If you are not mature in the Word of God, you will believe the lie and think that you are getting discernment from Him. True discernment comes from the sensitivity of knowing Christ with the help of the Holy Spirit. It comes from a place of deep love and spiritual maturity.

1 Corinthians 13 gives us the way we should behave when we have agape love. False discernment sees the outside of a person's situation. It is slow to hear, quick to speak, and quick to anger.

> *"Broods of vipers! How can you, being evil, speak good things? For out of the abundance of the heart the mouth speaks. A good man out of the good treasure of his heart brings forth good things, and an evil man out of the evil treasure brings forth evil things."*[109]

Discernment must go through a filter—the Word of God. If you think you are receiving revelations when praying for others, you must know what the Word of God says in order to discern those revelations. If the information you

---

109 Matthew 12:34–35 (NKJV)

are receiving in prayer is not in line with the scriptures, then it did not come from God. God does not cause you to sin. He shows you or tells you what to pray for when praying for others only when you are mature and able to discern with the fruit of the Holy Spirit.

True discernment comes with the manifestation of love and the right attitude. If negative information about someone is revealed to you in prayer, it is revealed so that you can pray for that person. If you reveal that negative information to someone else, that is gossiping. Gossiping is not pleasing to God. It is sin. As an intercessor, God does not reveal negative information to you about a person in order for you to think badly of them and cause you to sin. If the negative information you receive in your spirit causes you to hate or judge that person, then the information you received did not come from God.

Remember you are in spiritual warfare, and the enemy does not want you to succeed or help others to succeed. Keep your mind from going into places that will lead to evil thinking about someone. Evil spirits will come along and tempt you, and then they will stand back to see what you will do with the information they give you in your thoughts. If it keeps happening over a period of time and you accept it as truth, you have opened a door for the enemy to come and build a stronghold in your mind. You need to keep your mind on the Word of God so that you will not give place to evil spirits. Deepen your knowledge of the scriptures to live in one hundred percent victory over the enemy. Your victory is not automatic, it depends upon your relationship with God and His Word. Satan's objective is to deceive Man and lead Man into rebellion against God and His will for mankind. To keep your heart pure, the motivation behind every action must be love. Whatever you visualize in your mind must come out of love. There is a principle that as a person thinks in their heart, so they will become.

"For as he thinks in his heart, so is he."[110]

"Finally, brethren, whatsoever things are true, whatsoever things are noble, whatsoever things are just, whatsoever things are pure, whatsoever things are lovely, whatsoever things are of good report; if there is any virtue and if there is anything praiseworthy - meditate on these things."[111]

Satan uses what we withhold from God in our lives to deceive us. God said to him, "dust you shall eat all the days of your life."[112] Man was made from dust. This is the essence of the carnal nature of man. Our mind is carnal by nature, we were born in sin and shaped in iniquity. Satan hides in the ignorance of believers. When you do not know something, that is fertile ground for Satan to deceive and oppress you. Even though God loves us, He will not violate

---

110 Proverbs 23:7 (NKJV)
111 Philippians 4:8 (NKJV)
112 Genesis 3:14 (AMP)

His word. The enemy knows this and continues to hide in a believer's ignorance.

Knowledge of God's Word and repentance are the keys to being delivered from the enemy's strongholds. The way a person thinks can turn into habitual responses; addiction, compulsion, obsession, and chronic fear. This keeps them from believing the Word of truth. Where there is a sin-habit, it will become a dwelling place for an evil spirit to rob the believer of their blessings from God. Jesus said that Satan came to steal, kill, and destroy.

> *"The thief does not come except to steal, and to kill, and to destroy. I have come that they may have life, and that they may have it more abundantly."*[113]

Fortresses exist in thought-patterns and ideas that govern individuals. A person can be ignorant to the truth. This is called darkness. Darkness is not the absence of light, it is the absence of God, who is The Light.

> *"He has delivered us from the power of darkness and conveyed us into the kingdom of the Son of His love."*[114]

> *"Therefore, take heed that the light which is in you is not darkness."*[115]

---

113 John 10:10 (NKJV)
114 Colossians 1:13 (NKJV)
115 Luke 11:35 (NKJV)

Jesus said to "take heed," which means that the enemy can sow darkness in the heart of Man if Man is not watchful. When the believer harbors sin, the devil will be in that area of their heart. Willful disobedience will dim the believer's light. If a Christian doesn't have a prayer life, then he will not come into the divine truth and purity where God dwells.

A believer's thinking is important to walking in daily victory. Spiritual battles begin with our private thoughts, and they can only be won using spiritual weapons. As long as a believer is praying, they are in spiritual warfare. They are coming against the kingdom of darkness. We must gain control over our own minds by ensuring that every thought we have is in obedience with God's Word. Guard your thoughts.

PRAISE BREAK
Psalm 34:1

I will bless the Lord at all times, and His praise shall continually be in my mouth. With my hands lifted up and my mouth filled with praise, I bless You, Lord.

PRAYER
Father, I thank You for opening my eyes to the truth. Break off limitations and restrictions from my life that come from any evil spirit. I pull down any stronghold in my mind that does not line up with Your Word. I receive deliverance from every stronghold in my mind. I renounce all disobedience and rebellion from my life. I surrender my will so that Your will can be done in me. In Jesus Christ's Name. Amen 🙏

TAKE AWAY
- Your life will be a reflection of your mindset. The Word of God is the only agent that can transform the mind.
- A stronghold is a belief system in the mind where darkness reigns. It is a way of thinking that is rooted in a lie, but a person comes to believe it as being the truth.

Chapter 9

Generational Curses and Self-Deliverance

PLEASE DO NOT get offended as you read this chapter. If you do not agree with what you are about to read, God bless you, and thank you for picking up this book. Now, before we go any farther, here are some helpful definitions:

A *generation* is the circle of life that spans from a man's birth to that of his son; this period was reckoned to be forty years.[116] Time was commonly referred to in increments of generations in the context of blessings and curses.[117]/[118]

---

116 Numbers 32:13
117 Exodus 20:5
118 Eerdmans Bible Dictionary

A ***generation*** is a group of individuals born at the same time. The average time interval between the birth of parents and that of their offspring.[119]

A ***covenant*** is an agreement between two or more parties outlining mutual rights and responsibilities.[120]

A ***curse*** is the invocation of harm or injury upon a person or people, either immediately or contingent upon particular circumstances. It is a malediction or imprecation.[121]

I realize that some Christians do not believe in generational curses, and I know it's easy for a believer to say that generational curses do not affect someone after they are born again. From my own experiences, however, I have seen these cycles running through my family, even in those who are born again. Look at the evidence. The evidence tells the story. This is something that God has opened my eyes to. I had to go through self-deliverance to come to this truth. There were things that I was going through that I had to face in my walk with God. I was a Christian. I believed in God. Jesus was (and still is) my Lord and Savior. Yet I still had some setbacks and blocks in my path that I needed to deal with. After going through self-deliverance, I got my breakthrough.

---

119 Webster's Dictionary
120 Eerdmans Bible Dictionary
121 Eerdmans Bible Dictionary

When you have done all you can in prayer and know you are in right standing with God, yet you feel as if you are getting nowhere in your Christian walk, it is time to look closer at what is going on in the family bloodline to see if there are any cycles that could be generational curses.

Sometimes you can inherit (reap) things from others that you did not plan (sow) for your life. Inheriting wealth is a blessing, but what if you inherit the consequences of what someone did because of their greed? That is what a generational curse is—a sin nature that has been passed down from one generation to another. A generational curse is a law that is working through a bloodline, between a soul and a spirit other than the Holy Spirit. There are some causes that will help you to determine if there is a curse running in your family.

1. Someone in the bloodline went for help in the kingdom of darkness and made a covenant, resulting in a negative pattern following through the family.
2. Someone in authority spoke over your life using negative words, and you believe them to be truth. "For as he thinks in his heart, so is he in behavior."[122] You have soul-ties with someone you've partnered with (whether friendship or marriage) who has or had a curse on their life, which is also affecting your life. They may also be controlling you with a spirit other than the Holy Spirit.

---

122 Proverbs 23:7 (AMP)

3. You may have something in your house that was cursed. Evil spirits can be attached to cursed items.

Every family is like a tree. Look at the fruits that are produced in the family.

> *"For a good tree does not bear bad fruit,*
> *nor does a bad tree bear good fruits."*[123]

When someone goes to the kingdom of darkness for help, they are not just involving themselves, they are also involving the family bloodline. Satan makes covenants with generations, not just with the person who is involved. He wants to destroy entire generations, and only the blood of Jesus can stop him.

When it is a generational curse, you have to deal with the root, and not the symptoms. How do you know if you have a generational curse in your bloodline? There are symptoms that can help you identify if there is one in your family. Here are just a few:

1. Everyone in the family is experiencing the same sickness, disease, or chronic illness.
2. A number of family members have suffered from mental illness and emotional breakdowns.
3. Family members are not able to understand or concentrate on what they read in the Bible.
4. No one seems to get ahead. Every time someone receives a financial blessing or saves up, something

---
[123] Luke 6:43 (NKJV)

happens, and they are right back where they started. There is continued financial insufficiency.
5. There is a history of barrenness or miscarriages in the family.
6. Every time that family members try something, they fail. They live from one trial to the next, always being defeated.
7. Most family members experience divorce or unfaithfulness and abuse in their marriage.
8. There are a number of untimely or unnatural deaths and a history of suicides in the family.

There are evil spirits that are connected to these curses. When it is beyond human ability, deliverance is needed. God's Word is law, and it is the same yesterday, today, and forever. If you don't obey His command, or if you have any habitual sin in your life, then a door can be opened to the kingdom of darkness, even if it is done in ignorance. Satan works well in the believer's ignorance. These doors that are open to evil spirits can run through a family if no one renounces these curses in order to close them. These covenants are legal, which give the evil spirits legitimate grounds to attack.

> *"Don't be misled remember that you can't ignore God and get away with it, a man will always reap just the kind of crop he sows."[124]*

---

124 Galatians 6:7 (TLB)

Covenants that are made with evil spirits go through generations, running down the bloodline, negatively affecting a family. When you see certain cycles in your family, know that it is something more than the ordinary. You must pray and intercede about it. For example, several women in your family have miscarriages or infidelity in their marriages, many members have married multiple times, or a grandfather is an alcoholic, the father is an alcoholic, and then the son becomes an alcoholic. These are cycles that will go on for generations if no one stands in the gap and prays about them. Prayer is the only thing that can break these cycles in the bloodline. Generational curses have to be renounced so that the evil covenant can be broken over one's life. This is important.

The believer might say, "But Jesus became a curse for us and died for our sins so that we can be set free." That is true. However, we must look deeper and gain the required knowledge of how to take that freedom in Jesus Christ's Name.

> *"Christ has redeemed us from the curse of the law, having become a curse for us for it is written cursed is everyone who hangs on a tree."*[125]

Jesus defeated the power of Satan, not the presence of Satan. The power of the curse is broken, but someone has to exercise the authority over the curse. The believer has the ability to be free from bloodline curses by using the

---

125 Galatians 3:13 (NKJV)

authority that was given in Jesus' Name. Jesus became a curse for the believer and, therefore, we have the righteousness of Jesus.

Please remember Jesus told us to fight the good fight of faith. He said, "From the days of John the Baptist until now the Kingdom of Heaven has suffered violence, and the violent take it by force."[126] We are to fight in victory not for victory. We already have the victory through Christ. When Jesus said that the violent take it by force, he did not mean that the people in the Kingdom are violent literally, but rather their eagerness, relentlessness, and forcefulness in prayer, fasting and the things of God, is like an army demolishing fortresses. We have to fight the sin nature within us in order to stay victorious and break generational curses.

As you pray, the Holy Spirit will reveal if you are dealing with a generational curse or not. The believer's faith goes on trial, not the consequences of their eternal destination. To live a productive life the believer needs to go through life cleansed from all unrighteousness. We are saved through Jesus Christ's blood alone, by faith alone, through grace alone, so understand that while generational curses can affect the quality of a believer's life on earth, their salvation in Christ is not in question, meaning that they will still go to Heaven.

Some generational curses activate at different seasons in a person's life. A difficult conflict, trauma, or bad experience can wake up a curse. Generational curses can also be

---

126 Matthew 11:12 (English Standard Version)

dormant in a person's life until they come to Christ. A new believer can begin to experience challenges and setbacks. This is so the new Christian will give up and not continue in their faith. A mature believer can be enjoying their Christian walk when, suddenly and with no explanation, they begin to experience challenges that become cycles of defeat.

In my journey, I had to press relentlessly to break generational curses and take my inheritance in Christ Jesus. I had to do this by not just believing but by taking action though fasting and prayer, and then declaring what Jesus did on the cross for me. Please allow me to now pray for you:

> *Father, I pray that You would open the eyes of Your child's understanding as they have read this chapter. Give them knowledge and wisdom. Remove the limitations and restrictions placed on their life by any evil spirits. Father, as they read, I pray they will receive deliverance and enlightenment from Your Word. Let Your son or daughter increase in knowledge, for knowing the truth will set him or her free. If there is any sin in this person's life, I pray that You would lead them to repentance, for Your love is never ending. Reveal Yourself in this person. In Jesus Christ's Name. Amen*

PRAISE BREAK
Psalm 34:6

This poor man cried out, and the Lord heard him, and saved him out of all his troubles. We give God praise for His goodness and mercy. Hallelujah. Bless His wonderful name. May He shine His light on every dark area in our life, raise your voice, and ask God for mercy.

PRAYER
Father, I close all doors, gates, and portals in my life that are open to the kingdom of darkness over myself and my family. I acknowledge that there is sin in my family bloodline. I repent of my sins and renounce all ancestors' covenants. I break every demonic contract that my ancestors made with the kingdom of darkness. I renounce all the evil covenants and apply the blood of Jesus Christ on my life and family. Father, destroy every demonic altar that has on it my name and my family's name. I bind every unclean spirit and familiar spirit attached to my bloodline. I destroy all blood covenants that my family established with the kingdom of darkness in the Name of Jesus Christ of Nazareth. I destroy and renounce all covenants that I have made knowingly and unknowingly. I repent of every covenant that I have made knowingly and unknowingly in my dreams in the Name of Jesus Christ of Nazareth. I come in agreement with the New Covenant of Jesus Christ of Nazareth. I release myself and those under my authority from any curse over our lives right now in the Name of Jesus Christ of Nazareth. Amen.

TAKE AWAY
- Deliverance: What we inherit through our bloodline must bow to the blood of Jesus Christ and what He did on the cross. What you don't know can harm you.
- You are not guilty of your ancestors' sins, but you can be affected by them.

Chapter 10

Disobedience and Deliverance

THANK YOU FOR making it this far! Here we go…

As you pray, God will show you if there are things in your life that you need deliverance from. Jesus died for our sin and gave us the power to be free from the tricks of Satan, who is the prince of this world. Many Christians think that just because they are believers in Christ, they cannot be under a curse. This conception is wrong. Curses can manifest in a believer's life because of doors that are open as a result of disobedience. It doesn't matter if you are aware of it or not, the curse will run its course. As long as a door is open, the devil has access, and he will take the opportunity to come into a believer's life, often times remaining uncovered.

The nature of blessings and curses are supernatural; they carry the power of good for blessing and evil for curses. In

Deuteronomy chapter twenty-eight, the law of God gives us fourteen blessings and fifty-four curses. Both blessings and curses can be transferred or transmitted by words or by physical objects. What happens when you are reaping what someone else has sowed? You can enjoy the benefits of the wise choices someone made in their life, and the blessings flow to you. But what if you are suffering because of the wrong choices someone else made? There is a story in Joshua 9:1–21, continuing in 2 Samuel 21:1–6. I will give you the short version. You can read the full account in the Bible.

The Gibeonites were a nation that the Israelites were to war against. The Gibeonites knew that God was with the children of Israel, so they came up with a plan to save their lives. The Israelites made a covenant with the Gibeonites, not knowing that they were nearby. Three days after they made the covenant with the Gibeonites, the Israelites came to find out that the Gibeonites were their neighbors. The Israelites kept the promise they made because the oath was made before the Lord. Joshua did not inquire of God first before making this covenant, but the covenant still stood. Joshua and the Elders agreed that as long as they lived the Gibeonites would be their servants, and they would not go to war against them. After Joshua died, God raised up different judges in the land. The people of Israel looked at the other nations and saw they had kings ruling over them, so they asked God for a king. God answered and gave them King Saul. After the death of King Saul, David became the next King of Israel. King David experienced famine in the land for three years. He asked God why they were experiencing the famine, and God told King David that it was because King Saul broke the covenant by going to war and killing thousands of the Gibeonites. King David had to go to the Gibeonites and ask what could be done so that the famine could come to an end. The Gibeonites asked for seven sons of King Saul, and they hung them. After their deaths, the rain came down. The famine was over.

God didn't require human sacrifice, but because of the covenant Israel made with the Gibeonites three hundred years before, God told King David to go to them. King David agreed to the Gibeonites' request because of the broken covenant. God does not violate His law. When God says something, His words will not return to Him void.

> *"Therefore, know that the Lord is your God, He is God, the faithful God who keeps covenant and mercy for a thousand generations with those who love Him and keep His commandments."*[127]

> *"My covenant I will not break, nor alter the word that has gone out of My lips."*[128]

As discussed in the previous chapter, sin and iniquity can run through a family. Iniquity is the abuse of sin; a habitual habit. When the believer is consistently abusing sin without asking for forgiveness, this can come with

---

127 Deuteronomy 7:9 (NKJV)

128 Psalm 89:34 (NKJV)

heavy consequences. A believer who is experiencing the consequences of their own actions may not have a bloodline curse. The repercussions may have nothing to do with the family bloodline, just the individual. Please know that not all problems have an evil spirit behind them. Some difficulties are simply the result of a person's actions. For example, if a believer has sex outside of marriage and contracts an incurable sexually transmitted disease, they can ask God to forgive them for their sexual sin and their sin would be forgiven, but they would still have that incurable disease. Some sins carry heavy consequences.

> *"And you He made alive, who were dead in trespassed and sins, in which you once walked according to the course of this world, according to the prince of the power of the air, the spirit who now works in the sons of disobedience, among whom also we all once conducted ourselves in the lusts of our flesh fulfilling the desires of the flesh and of the mind, and were by nature children of wrath, just as the others."*[129]

A believer's spirit has been redeemed, but he still has to deal with his sinful nature. When a person has been born again, he becomes alive to the Spirit and the Word of God. The cross broke the power of the curse, but the believer must take authority over the curse.

---

129 Ephesians 2:1–3 (NKJV)

Although a believer's spirit has been redeemed and cannot be possessed, he can still be oppressed by an evil spirit. Evil spirits can influence a believer's thinking pattern, causing them to take certain harmful actions. They can also live in the outer part of Man's body, latching on to sickness, addiction, poverty, rejection, hatred, sexual sins, and other sinful natures.

For example, one day while working beside a colleague, we had a disagreement. She was upset and wouldn't let go of her anger. This co-worker was a person who seemed to be angry most of the time. I tried not to let it bother me, but I felt anger on the inside, and it lasted until I got home. Two of my pet peeves are dirty dishes in the sink after a certain length of time and shoes being in disarray at the door. Well, when I got home that day, the shoes were in disarray at the door and the sink was filled with dirty dishes. I got very angry and decided that when my kids got home, I was really going to let them have it. Then, as I started to wash the dishes, I began to think, "Why am I so upset?" I had one angry thought rolling into another. As I began to tell myself that there was no need to be so angry, I saw a shadow lift off of me and go through the door. This encounter taught me that sometimes when we're having a prevailing thought that does not stop, we are under attack from evil spirits. You have to stay proactive about what you are thinking about.

The believer's soul and body still have the sinful nature that must be submitted to God before they can experience total victory in every area of their life. As previously discussed, the soul is made up of the mind, will, and emotions. God impresses on us, but he does not override our will.

Having to deal with sickness, demons, and curses is the result of the sinful nature. Jesus broke the power of the curse, but the believer must stay active and take authority over it. The only way a curse can work in a believer's life is when the believer is in habitual sin and not repentant. This opens a door for evil spirits to enter their life. No one can curse the believer when they are in right standing with God. Someone can go ahead with their curse, but it will not affect them.

> *"How shall I curse whom God has not cursed? And how shall I denounce whom the Lord has not denounced?"*[130]

There has to be an existing curse or a violation on the believer's part for the curse to run its course. If the believer is living a holy life, no curse can harm him or her.

> *"Like a flitting sparrow, like a flying swallow, so a curse without cause shall not alight."*[131]

God doesn't set you free from a curse simply because He loves you, He sets you free because justice has been satisfied. God is love, and God is just. Jesus' blood satisfied

---

[130] Numbers 23:4 (NKJV)
[131] Proverbs 26:2 (NKJV)

God's hunger. God loves His children regardless of our sin, but we must meet the conditions He set out in His Word.

> *"Yet it pleased the Lord to bruise Him (Jesus), He (God) has put Him (Jesus) to grief when you make His (Jesus) soul an offering for sin. He shall see His seed (Jesus will rise from the dead), He shall prolong His days (He will live forever), and the pleasure of the Lord shall prosper in His hand. He (God) shall see the labor of His (Jesus) soul, and be satisfied."*[132]

Disobedience causes curses, and curses give demons a legal right to attack the believer. God decrees the curses because of disobedience. Demons carry out the curses. When the law of God has been violated whether willfully or in ignorance, Satan has legal grounds for the curse to run its course. Ignorance (or not knowing) will not stop the curse.

Read the story in the Book of Joshua, chapter seven. This is the short version:

Achan disobeyed God's command and took what God said was a curse. Because of one man's sin, the children of Israel lost thousands of men in the war against Ai. God's penalty was to stone Achan, his wife, his children, and his livestock to death.

In this story, Achan was the one who sinned, but his family and livestock paid the penalty. Satan is enforcing the

---

132 Isaiah 53:10–11 (NKJV)

penalty for the disobedience and violation of the command of the law of God. God's penalty for the violation is to allow the curse to run its course. Only the blood of Jesus can break the curse.

> *"The word of the Lord came to me again, saying, What do you mean when you use this proverb concerning the land of Israel, saying: The fathers have eaten sour grapes, and the children's teeth are set on edge? As I live, says the Lord God, you shall no longer use this proverb in Israel. Behold all souls are Mine; the soul of the father as well as the soul of the son is Mine; the soul who sins shall die."*[133]

God was rebuking the people of Judah for not acknowledging their own guilt. They were idolatrous, they oppressed their slaves, they were not obeying the commandments of God, and they were blaming their forefathers for the judgment of God. Judgment goes according to individual conduct and faith. The reason these kinds of curses run this course is because of individual sin.

Whenever you are under a non-stop spiritual attack, there could be a spiritual valuation. Sometimes God removes the hedge of protection around the believer so that they can mature in their walk with Him. In those cases the spiritual attack is not necessarily a curse. That is why it is so important to fast and pray, asking the Holy Spirit for discernment so that you can rightly understand

---
[133] Ezekiel 18:1–4 (NKJV)

the problem or situation you are dealing with. You have to be able to discern what you are dealing with so as not to misjudge the situation.

Curses can also come when you partake in certain activities. Some examples are:
1. Practicing and engaging with forbidden occult objects or images, like Ouija boards.
2. Using supernatural abilities that are not from the Word of God or the Holy Spirit.
3. Speaking with psychics and participating in palm readings.
4. Practicing any kind of magic—good or bad.
5. Not being careful about what you are putting into your mind. For example, having a love for violence in movies, having an appetite for evil actions in movies, or viewing pornography.
6. Placing importance in astrology and possessing crystals or good luck charms.

The evil spirits attached to these objects and activities are invisible to the natural eye, but they are real. You can see the effects they have on people's lives. God has given us everything we need to destroy the works of the kingdom of darkness. When a person is ignorant to Satan's devices, they will stay defeated and believe that life should just be that way.

In the Book of Job, chapter one, Job did not know why he was going through hardship, and he was fearful. When God removed the hedge from around him, his fears came through. God protects His children until they are mature enough to overcome difficult temptations. He doesn't allow any temptation to overtake us beyond our ability.

> *"Now I say that the heir, as long as he is a child, is different from a servant, though he be lord of all, but is under tutors and governors until the time appointed by the father."*[134]

A person living for Christ can still experience a cycle of defeat, living in poverty, battling addiction, or experiencing sickness throughout his life. Only the blood of Jesus and the authority of the Word of God can break the power of evil over the believer's life. They can declare and decree the Word of God over their lives, but they must obey His commands before they can change the effects and the quality of their life. The believer must renounce the evil spirits that are influencing their actions and feelings. When a Christian is unable to break free from addiction, this is an indication that an evil spirit may be attached to his members.

> *"But I see another law in my members, warring against the law of my mind, and bringing me into captivity to the law of sin which is in my members".*[135]

---

134 Galatians 4:1–2 (KJV)
135 Romans 7:23 (KJV)

Here, the Apostle Paul is talking about the sin nature, but the believer must submit his body to Christ so that his members don't become a slave to sin. Habitual sin can attract evil spirits, therefore, a believer must live a life that is holy before God. No one can live this way on their own. All have sinned and fallen short of the glory of God. We need the help of the Holy Spirit to regenerate us.

An unbeliever can be possessed by an unclean spirit and come under its control. The believer can go through the same things as the unbeliever, but the unclean spirit cannot possess them. As discussed earlier, Man has three parts to his makeup: the spirit, soul, and body. Evil spirits, unclean spirits, and demons can't infiltrate the believer's spirit, but the believer can be influenced by them through addictions and unrepented sins.

Demons, unclean spirits, and evil spirits are all from the kingdom of darkness. There are different levels or ranking of these spirits without bodies that are looking for a body to enter.

Evil spirits are to be cast out, and not pulled down. When in prayer, remember to cast out the demons in Jesus Christ's Name. Pull down the stronghold by replacing the lie with the truth of the Word of God. When a believer is vulnerable to a temptation, that person can become an easy target for the enemy. Believers are being attacked consistently every day. We must guard our minds with God's Word.

Rejection, rebellion, and the root of bitterness can open the door for strongholds to be built up in the mind. These strongholds can become open doors for unclean spirits and demons to enter if not pulled down. Through the work on the cross of Jesus Christ, we are transitioned from the kingdom of darkness into the kingdom of light. This transition will take an act of faith on the believer's part. It will not just happen. The believer must actively take part in their transformation by the renewing of their mind. We must make a choice. Because of free will, we can choose to believe in God or in our own abilities. When we choose to believe in God, that brings about His goodness in our lives. He shall know the truth, and knowing the truth will set you free.

> *"And do not be conformed to this world but be transformed by the renewing of your mind, that you may prove what is that good and acceptable and perfect will of God."*[136]

So how can you be released or delivered from curses?
1. Confess your faith in Jesus Christ of Nazareth.
2. Commit yourself to obedience to the Word of God.
3. Confess known sins of yourself and ancestors. The sins of your ancestors sometimes affect you. You are not guilty of or responsible for your ancestor's sins, but you can be affected by them. If you know your ancestors were involved in idol worship, release yourself from it.

---

136 Romans 12:2 (NKJV)

4. Forgive all people that wronged or hurt you. Forgiving someone is not about your emotions, it's a decision you make to obey God's command. You are giving God access in your life and removing the barriers of bitterness in order to receive the blessings from God.
5. Renounce all contact with the occult for yourself and your ancestors.
6. Get rid of occult objects from your home.

Confess and expect the blessings of the Lord. You must continue to be obedient and confess your faith in Him. Here are some Bible verses surrounding your release and deliverance:

Ephesians 1:7 (NKJV)
In Him we have redemption through His blood, the forgiveness of sins, according to the riches of His grace.

Colossians 1:13–14 (NKJV)
He has delivered us from the power of darkness and conveyed us into the kingdom of the Son of His love, in whom we have redemption through His blood the forgiveness of sins.

---

1 John 3:8 (NKJV)
He who sins is of the devil, for the devil has sinned from the beginning. For this purpose, the Son of God was manifested, that He might destroy the works of the devil.

Luke 10:19 (NKJV)
Behold, I give you the authority to trample on serpents and scorpions, and over all the power of the enemy and nothing shall by any means hurt you.

Galatians 3:13—14 (NKJV)
Christ has redeemed us from the curse of the law, having become a curse for us for it is written cursed is everyone who hangs on a tree. That the blessing of Abraham might come upon the Gentiles in Christ Jesus, that we might receive the promise of the Spirit through faith.

PRAISE BREAK
Psalm 37:39

But the salvation of the righteous is from the Lord. He is their strength in the time of trouble. Who can stand against the Lord? No one can! I will Praise You with everything that I am.

PRAYER

Father, I take back the territories from the kingdom of darkness that were in my life. Lord Jesus Christ, I believe that you are the Son of God and the only way to the Father. I believe you died on the cross for my sin and rose again from the dead. On the cross you were made a curse for me. Lord, I confess any sin committed by me or by my ancestors that has brought a curse on my life. I ask for your forgiveness. I also forgive all those who harmed or wronged me. I speak to the spirit of rejection, abandonment, pride, fear, witchcraft, poverty, sickness (name the spirit of the trouble you are dealing with) to come out. I take authority over (name the spirit or spirits) and command them to stop their assignment in my life. I break the curse off my life, family, and children in the Name of Jesus Christ of Nazareth. I receive it by faith. Father, you put all my sin on Jesus when He was nailed on the cross. Jesus disarmed all principalities and powers when He made a public spectacle of them, triumphing over them. I thank you for the victory and the forgiveness of sin. I have a new life in Christ. Baptize me with your Holy Spirit. Father, I ask for grace, for favor, and for wisdom to obtain my Godly inheritance in Jesus Christ's Name. Father, I pray for restoration for the years of failure in my life. I know that You are able to keep me from falling. I give You all the praise and glory. Let Your kingdom come and Your will be done in my life. In the Name of Jesus Christ. Amen.

TAKE AWAY

- Disobedience causes curses to activate and demons to carry out attacks on the believer on legal grounds (according to God's laws).
- Rejection, rebellion, and the root of bitterness can open doors to strongholds in the mind of the believer.
- We pull down strongholds and cast out demons.
- You can be delivered from curses through the knowledge of who you are in Christ Jesus.

Chapter 11

The Last Will and Testament of Jesus Christ

> *"But ye shall receive power, after that the Holy Ghost is come upon you; and ye shall be witnesses unto me both in Jerusalem, and in all Judaea, and in Samaria, and unto the uttermost part of the earth."*[137]

THESE WERE JESUS' last words to His disciples. He told them that they would be His witnesses. For them to be effective witnesses they needed to wait until they received the power from the Holy Spirit. They couldn't be effective by themselves. They needed help. Jesus wanted them to have an encounter with the Holy Spirit so that they would be empowered.

When you are convicted of the truth, you are able to speak with certainty of what you witness. The Holy Spirit's ministry to the believer is to reveal, conform, and guide

---

137 Acts 1:8 (KJV)

Men in the truth of the Word of God. The encounter with the person of the Holy Spirit was needed to strengthen the disciples' faith and give them power for the ministry.

> *"After that He was seen of above five hundred brethren at once; of whom the greater part remain unto this present, but some are fallen asleep."*[138]

Jesus appeared to more than five hundred people after His resurrection. He instructed them to wait until they received the power of His Spirit. This was very important to carry out the commandment of going into all the world to preach the gospel. The disciples were to become witnesses before they could leave Jerusalem. The power transformed Peter from a coward to a courageous spokesman for God. Jesus' command has not changed. We too need the power of the Holy Spirit to transform our lives as well to become witnesses for Jesus Christ.

A Christian life is a testimony of what Jesus has done in that life. The transformation is recognized in the way we love others and in the way we live for God. Jesus gives a command to His disciples, but they can only accomplish it by receiving the power of the Holy Spirit and allowing Him to work in their lives. The command to go into all the world and preach the gospel could not be done in their own strength. It is the same for believers today. We need the baptism of the Holy Spirit.

---

138 1 Corinthians 15:6 (BRG Bible)

The disciples witnessed the teachings of Jesus. They lived, talked, and ate with Christ for three and a half years. They heard the teachings and preaching of the Kingdom of God. Jesus taught His discipleship how to live a victorious life by being an example Himself.

The four gospels give us the record of the lifestyle a believer should live. Through Man, God has established His Kingdom on the earth. Man disobeyed God's command and lost the authority that was given to him. Jesus came and lived a righteous life, then died for the sins of Man so that Man could be made right with the Father again.

> *"For God so loved the world that He gave His only begotten Son, that whoever believes in Him should not perish but have everlasting life."*[139]

The sermons of Jesus Christ teach us how we should live and love in the Kingdom of God:

1. **Lifestyle of a believer:** The sermons of Jesus give us the keys we need to understand how the principles of the Kingdom of God work. Jesus taught us how to live our daily lives in the Kingdom. He showed us how to pray to the Father. The sermons teach the believer how to live with others in the Kingdom, who is qualified to be in the Kingdom, and who will inherit the Kingdom.
2. **Mission of a believer:** Wherever Jesus went He was healing the sick and casting out demons.

---
139 John 3:16 (NKJV)

He gave His disciples authority to cast out evil spirits and heal every kind of sickness and disease. Jesus preached with a demonstration of how the Kingdom of God operated. He also gave the disciples the opportunity to preach about the Kingdom of God.

3. **Growth of a believer:** Jesus taught the disciples how the Kingdom would grow and what soil would bring in the most harvest. When the Word of God is sowed into the heart of a soul, the results may not be immediate, but we must continue to sow until He returns and receives the harvest.

4. **The community of a believer:** Jesus taught how the Kingdom functions within the body. He explained that the Kingdom is like a little child who humbles himself and that when two or more agree on earth in His Name He will be in the midst to bless them. He taught that believers must forgive one another or the Heavenly Father will not forgive their sin or hear them when they pray.

5. **Future of a believer:** Jesus told His disciples that false prophets will come claiming to be the Messiah and lead many astray. The love of many will grow cold. Jesus warned that the believer should be watchful because no one knows the time or the hour when He will return.

All of these truths were given to the disciples, yet Jesus' last words to them were to stay in Jerusalem until they received the power of the Holy Spirit. To receive the power, they had to obey. Like us today, we need the Holy Spirit to transform us into the likeness of Christ. In salvation there is:

1. **Atonement:** A change of relationship with God. "For if when we were enemies we were reconciled to God through the death of His Son, much more, having been reconciled, we shall be saved by His life. And not only that but we also rejoice in God through our Lord Jesus Christ, through whom we have now received the reconciliation."[140]
2. **Redemption:** A change of ownership. "In Him we have redemption through His blood, the forgiveness of sins, according to the riches of His grace."[141]
3. **Faith:** A change of attitude toward God. "But without faith it is impossible to please Him, for he who comes to God must believe that He is and that He is a rewarder of those who diligently seek Him."[142]
4. **Repentance:** A change of mind about God.
   4.a Conviction of sin: A sense of guilt. Your conscience comes alive by the Word of God.
   4.b Godly sorrow: Knowing you grieved God by your wrong doing.
   4.c Confession: When you are truly sorry, you are willing to confess past wrongs.

---
140 Romans 5:10–11 (NKJV)
141 Ephesians 1:7 (NKJV)
142 Hebrews 11:6 (NKJV)

    4.d Restitution: Whenever possible, we will make our wrongs right.

    4.e Forsaking sin: You stop sinning.

5. **Justification:** A change of standing before God. "Much more than having now been justified by His blood We shall be saved from wrath through Him." [143]

6. **Conversion:** A change of life. "Among whom also we all once conducted ourselves in the lusts of our flesh fulfilling the desires of the flesh and of the mind and were by nature children of wrath, just as the others."[144]

7. **Regeneration:** A change of nature. "Do not marvel at what I said to you, you must be born again."[145]

8. **Adoption:** A change of family. "For as many as are led by the Spirit of God, these are sons of God. For you did not receive the spirit of bondage again to fear, but you received the Spirit of adoption by whom we cry out Abba Father."[146]

9. **Sanctification:** A change of service. "Therefore, if anyone cleanses himself from the latter, he will be a vessel for honor, sanctified and useful for the Master, prepared for every good word."[147]

---

[143] Romans 5:9 (NKJV)

[144] Ephesians 2:3 (NKJV)

[145] John 3:7 (NKJV)

[146] Romans 8:14–15 (NKJV)

[147] 2 Timothy 2:21 (NKJV)

A believer who lives and walks with God, must transform. Jesus said, "If any man comes after Me, he must deny himself and take up his cross daily and follow Me. For whoever wants to save his life will lose it, but whoever will lose his life for my sake, the same shall save it."[148]

How would you react if your country was taken over by another nation and you were forced to pay taxes? How would you process it? This is what the disciples were facing. Living in Jesus' days, knowing that Jesus was the King of all kings and had the power to reign as king, yet He refused to come against the Romans. The Romans occupied their land, and they were forced to pay taxes.[149] The Roman government was oppressing the people of God. They wanted relief from their oppressors, but Jesus told them that only by losing their lives would they find abundant life. This couldn't be done by human nature. They needed the power of the Holy Spirit, just like we do today.

The truth of what a person believes will show up in how he lives. When a believer lives to obey God, the Holy Spirit will strengthen him to endure hard times. The Spirit helps the believer in times of weakness when he does not know what to pray for. The power to live a holy life comes from the Holy Spirit. He will put you in check when you are going in the wrong direction.

---

148 Luke 9:23--24 (Authorized King James Version)
149 Matthew 17:24-26 (NKJV)

PRAISE BREAK
Luke 1:46

My soul magnifies the Lord and my spirit has rejoiced in God, my salvation. Thank you, Lord, for Your mercy and grace.

PRAYER
Father, thank You for giving Your son Jesus Christ to die for my sin. Thank You for Your Holy Spirit that comes to teach us and guide us. I ask for the Holy Spirit to baptize me so that I can be regenerated into your image. Let the fruit of the Holy Spirit manifest in my life. Draw me closer to You day by day so that I can be a witness for You. In Jesus Christ's Name. Amen. 🙏

TAKE AWAY
- Jesus' commandment to His followers is to wait for the Holy Spirit before getting into ministries. The Holy Spirit is the one who transforms our lives.

Chapter 12

Come into Agreement with God

JESUS PROMISES TO be present where two or three witnesses gather together in His name. Knowing this, there should be a sense of honor and reverence when we gather.

> *"For where two or three are gathered together in My name I am there in the midst of them."*[150]

If we become afraid of others, we will not give God the reverence that He deserves. When we gather together in Jesus' Name, we begin to conquer fear and bring God praise and glory.

The believer's loyalty should only be to Jesus. Do not get carried away by someone's charisma or their title in the House of God. It is easy to fall into idolatry; worshiping

---

150 Matthew 18:20 (NKJV)

a person rather than Jesus. You must know God for yourself. Know what the Word of God says about you. God has already provided for you in Christ Jesus, but you must agree with what God says about you. He gives the promises, but it takes faith on the believer's part to enter into the agreement. The decisions the believer makes will determine how long it will take for them to mature in Christ.

Salvation is there for the asking. Focus on God, and not people. You can ask for advice, but remember you must make your own choice. Only you will stand before God one day to give an account of what you did with the life that He gave to you.

> *"Therefore, having been justified by faith we have peace with God through our Lord Jesus Christ through whom also we have access by faith into this grace in which we stand and rejoice in hope of the glory of God. And not only that we also glory in tribulations knowing that tribulation produces perseverance and perseverance character and character hope. Now hope does not disappoint because the love of God has been poured out in our hearts by the Holy Spirit who was given to us."*[151]

Peter, one of Jesus' disciples, is a good example of when the Spirit of God is empowering a believer. Peter denied Jesus three times, but when he was empowered by the Holy Spirit, he stood and preached, leading thousands to believe

---

151 Romans 5:1–5 (NKJV)

in the Lord Jesus Christ and be baptized.[152] As someone learns to love Jesus, His priorities become more and more important in their life. A believer demonstrates their love for Christ by the way they live, and not just by the words they speak.

The Book of Acts, chapter ten, tells the story of God speaking to Peter in a dream, where He began to change Peter's perception of Gentile people. Peter, in his mind, divided the animal kingdom into two groups: clean and unclean. He had also put people into two categories: the righteous and the unrighteous. God impressed on Peter's heart that all people need the Good News and the power of the Holy Spirit. As Peter obeyed God, he saw the power of God fall on Cornelius and other Gentiles.

Jesus came into the world to show us what the Father looked like and, in turn, we are here to show the world what Jesus looks like. When we love one another, the unbeliever will see what the Kingdom of Heaven looks like. Jesus said, "By this all will know that you are My disciples, if you have love for one another."[153] To be disciples of Jesus, we must love one another. The believer must have the power of the Holy Spirit to love the way God loves.

The greatest gift that you can give someone is agape love. "Agape" is a Greek word meaning unconditional and self-less. Paul describes this kind of love in action.[154] Love is understood by how it acts, not by how it feels. The Spirit

---

152 Acts 2:14–38 (NKJV)
153 John 13:35 (NKJV)
154 1 Corinthians 13 (NKJV)

of God gives us this love when we surrender our lives to Christ. It manifests as one of the characters of the fruit of the Holy Spirit. Love is patient, it is slow to anger, and it is tolerant. Love is kind. It benefits others. It finds a way to extend wellness to enemies. Love is not jealous. When love looks at someone who is more gifted or popular, it rejoices. Love doesn't brag. It is not self-centered. Love is not arrogant. It is not high minded. Finally, love cares about others.

> *"But the fruit of the Spirit is love, joy, peace, longsuffering, kindness, goodness, faithfulness, gentleness, self-control. Against such there is no law."*[155]

Godly attitudes characterize the spiritual kingdom of redeemed people in life-giving churches. The Holy Spirit produces fruit in believers, which have nine characteristics, as indicated in the verse above. They are:

1. **Love**: Humble concern for others more than yourself. Self-sacrificial service. It is not emotional affection. It is a choice you make to love. (1 John 3:16–17)
2. **Joy**: Happiness based on unchanging divine promises. It is a gift from God. Others can feel it and take on your joy when they are near you. (1 Peter 1:8)
3. **Peace**: The inner calm that results from confidence in your relationship with the Lord. (Romans 8:28)
4. **Longsuffering**: Steadfastness in the midst of trials or deep disappointment. The ability to endure

---

[155] Galatians 5:22–23 (NKJV)

injuries inflicted by others and willingness to accept painful situations. (1 Timothy 1:15–16)
5. **Kindness:** Tender concern for others who are weaker or less compatible with you. (2 Timothy 2:24)
6. **Goodness:** Seeking the well-being of others over your own. (2 Thessalonians 1:11)
7. **Faithfulness**: Loyalty and trustworthiness in the ability of God. Continually believing in the unseen without giving up. (Lamentations 3:22)
8. **Gentleness**: Having a humble and gentle attitude in times of offense. The believer submits to God and resists the temptation of the devil. (James 1:22, Ephesians 4:2–3)
9. **Self-control**: Mastering your passions and desires. (2 Peter 1:5–6, 1 Corinthians 9:25)

A believer can be operating in the gifts of God and not have a relationship with Him. We do not qualify for the gifts; they are given to us. We receive them by faith. The gifts will fade away, but our character is what will last forever, and the greatest characteristic is love. Our gifts make room for us, but it is our character that holds us in position.

> *"And above all things have fervent love for one another, for love will cover a multitude of sins."*[156]

---

156 1 Peter 4:8 (NKJV)

PRAISE BREAK
Psalm 63:3

Because Your love and kindness are better than life, my lips shall always praise You. I rejoice in You, my Lord.

PRAYER
Father, thank You for Your grace and Your mercy. I ask for Your Holy Spirit to dwell inside of me and for my life to manifest your love, joy, peace, long-suffering, kindness, goodness, faithfulness, gentleness, and self-control. Have Your way in me. In Jesus' Name. Amen. 🙏

TAKE AWAY
- The Father has already provided for us in Christ Jesus, but we must agree with what God's Word says about us.

Chapter 13

Praying the Word of God

PRAYING THE WORD of God is praying prophetically. Praying prophetically is when God inspires you and leads you to a certain scripture for a specific situation. The Book of Psalms is a good place to start when wanting to pray the words of God. Just pray His words back to Him.

> *"So shall My word be that goes forth from My mouth it shall not return to Me void but it shall accomplish what I please. And it shall prosper in the thing for which I sent it."*[157]

When God speaks, He obligates Himself to obey His words. Speak into your life using the Word of God. Recite

---

157 Isaiah 55:11 (NKJV)

what God says about the circumstance that you are going through. God honors His Word above His Name.

> *"For you have magnified Your word above all Your name."*[158]

Satan will try to steal your authority by bringing temptation into your life, looking for a place to operate. When you submit to his temptation, this will take you out of alignment with God. Only the Word of God is able to bring you back into alignment. Getting familiar with the scriptures will give you the advantage when Satan brings temptations.

Remember, prayer is not the responsibility of spiritual leaders and those you look up to. God is looking for you to pray and have a relationship with Him. You can come into agreement with someone in faith when praying about a certain situation, but do not leave your prayer life in someone else's hands. Be excited to receive answers from the Lord when you pray.

Examples of Praying the Word of God

WHEN IN FEAR:
(Psalm 27, Psalm 23, 2 Timothy)
Lord, You are my light and my salvation. Whom shall I fear? You are the strength of my life. Of whom shall I be afraid? When the wicked and my enemies come against

---

[158] Psalm 138:2b (NKJV)

me to eat up my flesh, they will stumble and fall. They may encamp around me, but my heart will not fear. When war rises against me, I will be confident in You because you are my Shepherd, and I will not want for anything. You lead and guide me in green pastures. You restore my soul. Though I am walking through the valley of the shadow of death, I will fear no evil because You are with me. Your rod and staff comfort me. Father, You have not given me a spirit of fear. You give me power over the enemy, love to be kind to others, and a sound mind so that I can worship you in spirit and truth. (Now, add your own words and always end with, "In Jesus' Name. Amen.")

WHEN IN PAIN:
(Isaiah 53:5, Hebrews 11:6)
Father, I come to You because You alone are able to take this pain away. Jesus was wounded for my transgressions, He was bruised for my iniquities, the chastisement for my peace was upon Him, and by His stripes I was healed. I believe what Your Word says about You. You are my healer. I come to You in faith. You said, he that comes to You must believe that you are a rewarder of those who diligently seek You. (Now, add your own words and always end with, "In Jesus' Name. Amen.")

TIMES OF JOY:
(Psalm 34, Psalm 100)
I bless You, Lord. Your praise will continually be in my mouth. I boast of Your blessings. They are new every

morning. Great is Your faithfulness. I magnify You and exalt You. I enter Your gates with thanksgiving and Your courts with praise. I am so thankful for all Your blessings. You are a good God, and Your mercy is everlasting. You reign on high. Strength, glory, and honor all belong to you. (Now add your own words of love and praise to Him.)

WHEN YOU NEED MERCY:
(Psalm 51, Psalm 19, 1 John 2:1–2)
Father, have mercy on me. You are filled with love and kindness, and You are tender in mercy. Forgive me for my transgressions. Wash me in the blood of Jesus. Cleanse me from my sins. I know that I have sinned and come short of Your glory, but Your word says that You are faithful and just to forgive us when we sin. Your judgments are true and righteous. Let sin not have dominion over me. Keep me from evil. Let the words of my mouth and the meditation of my heart be acceptable in Your sight. You are my strength, my Lord, and my Redeemer. (Now pour out your heart to Him and end with, "In Jesus' Name. Amen.")

FOR PROTECTION:
(Psalm 91, Isaiah 54:17)
Father, King of Glory, the only true and living God. There is none to compare You with. The heavens declare Your glory. All things were made for Your glory. I was made for Your glory. No weapon fashioned against me will come to pass. It is my heritage to condemn those negative words spoken against me. I am dwelling under Your protection. You are

my refuge and strength. My confidence is in You. You are my shield and protector. No pestilence, no arrows of the enemy, no destruction will come near me in my dwelling place. Your angels encamp around me and keep me from all harm. You give me authority to trample upon lions and serpents in the invisible realm. You will keep me in times of trouble. You are my Salvation. In Jesus' Name. Amen.

WHEN GRIEVING FOR YOUR LOSS
(Psalms 39:12, Matthew 11:29–30)

Hear my prayer, oh Lord, and give ear to my cry. Do not be silent of my tears. Let me feel Your presence near me. I give this burden of loss to You, Lord. You said, "Come to Me all you who labor and are burdened, and I will give you rest. Take My yoke upon you and learn from Me, for I am meek and humble of heart, and you will find rest for yourselves, for My yoke is easy, and My burden is light." Help me to find rest in You and know that this too will pass. (Add your own words to tell God how you feel. End with, "In Jesus Christ's Name. Amen.")

IN TIMES OF SADNESS
(Psalm 61:1–5)

Oh Lord, listen to my cry, hear my prayer from the ends of the earth as I cry to You for help. When my heart is overwhelmed, lead me to the towering rock of safety, for You are my safe refuge, a fortress, where my enemies cannot reach me. Let me live forever in Your sanctuary, safe and sound. I need the shelter of Your wings, for You have heard my vows, O God. You have given me an inheritance, reserved for those who fear You. My soul is longing for Your presence. Lord, strengthen me, according to Your Word. Keep me from sinking deeper into sorrow. I put my hope and trust in You. Let Your Word light my path. (Continue to add your own words. End with, "In Jesus Christ's Name. Amen.")

WHEN IN ANGER
(Ephesians 4:26)
Father, Your Word says, "Be angry, yet do not sin; do not let the sun go down on your anger." I am having a very difficult time letting go of my anger. I want to obey Your Word. Please help me to let go of this anger inside of me. Help me to grow in Your grace and mercy and not let my emotions control me. I trust in Your Word. I know that You are able to keep me from falling into this temptation every time. Loose me from under the power of anger. (Continue adding your own words. End with, "In Jesus Christ's Name. Amen.")

WHEN YOU NEED FORGIVENESS
(1 John 1:9)
Father, You said in Your Word that if we confess our sin, You are faithful and just to forgive us and purify us from all unrighteousness. Search my heart for any unconfessed sin. I repent of my sins and receive Your forgiveness. I ask for strength so that I will not fall into the enemy's trap.

(You can continue your confessions in your own words. End with, "In Jesus Christ's Name. Amen.")

WHEN IN DOUBT OF YOUR SALVATION
(Romans 8:1, 8:35, Ephesians 1:4)
Thank You, Lord, for salvation. Your Word said there is therefore now no condemnation to those who are in Christ Jesus, who do not walk according to the flesh, but according to the Spirit. Strengthen me by Your Spirit to know that You are always present with me. According to Your Word, nothing is able to separate me from Your love. No tribulation, no distress, no prosecution, no famine, or any other thing can separate Your love from me. I have been chosen in Christ before the foundation of the world that I should be holy and without blame before You. I have boldness and access to You, Father, because of Christ Jesus. Thank you, Lord for Your goodness and mercy. In Jesus Christ's Name. Amen. 🙏

TO RELEASE YOURSELF FROM THE PAST
(Matthew 18:18, Isaiah 52:2)
Father, in the Name of Jesus Christ, I release myself from all past relationships that You did not ordain for me. I release myself from the effects of being controlled, manipulated, and dominated by past relationships. I release my mind from every mental bondage, fantasy, lust, and evil thinking. I release the members of my body and my five senses that were under the control of the enemy. I repent of all my sins and surrender my will to You. I renew my covenant

with You and receive Your forgiveness. In the Name of Jesus Christ. Amen. 🙏

WHEN IN WARFARE
(Psalm 91:120)

Father, I come to You in the Name of Jesus Christ. I do not fight against my brothers and sisters, but against evil spirits. You said 1000 shall fall at my side and 10,000 at my right hand, but it shall not come near me. You promised to keep me in all my ways and to bear me up in Your hands. You are my keeper. The sun will not harm me by day nor the moon by night. You will preserve me in my going out and in my coming in. You defeated the enemy and gave me the victory. I stand upon Your victory and take back every ground that the enemy stole from me. I root out from my life everything that does not exalt You. I come into agreement with Your will for my life. (Add your own words and end with, "In Jesus Christ's Name. Amen.")

PRAYER POINTS

Use as many of these prayer points as you would like, to assist you when you pray.

1. Raise me up to be a true witness.
2. Multiply Your grace and peace.
3. Father, let Your grace for favor be upon my life.
4. I am available. Make me usable.
5. I repent for my ignorance. Open my eyes to understanding Your will for my life.

6. Give me new dimensions of wisdom, knowledge, and understanding.
7. Give me a new beginning in my spiritual life.
8. Let me flow in the gifts of the Spirit.
9. Give me fresh seasons of grace and prophetic revelations.
10. Give me grace for speed. No more delay.
11. Open doors that are closed. Open gates to receive Your favor.
12. Supply anointing and prosperity over my life and family.
13. Purify motives in every area of life.
14. Help me to rise higher in prayer and to be more committed in prayer.
15. I pray for courage and boldness in Christ.
16. I pray to know the voice of God clearly.
17. I pray to be obedient to the Word of God.
18. I pray for spiritual wisdom.
19. I pray for a hunger to read and understand God's Word.
20. I pray healing for the physical body.
21. I pray to have a personal revival.
22. I pray for a national revival.
23. I pray to purify and strengthen Your love in our fellowship.
24. I pray for discernment to know the false prophets from the true prophets.
25. I pray for You to intervene in families of spiritual and worldly leaders.

26. I pray for a harvest of souls to come into the Kingdom of God.
27. I pray for doors to be opened to receive Jesus Christ.
28. I pray for the fulfilment of Bible prophecy and the return of Jesus Christ.
29. I pray for the sick, the homeless, the fatherless, and the motherless.
30. I pray for unity in the body of Christ.
31. I pray for the favor of God for evangelism.
32. I pray for the heart of Man to be receptive to hear the Word of God.
33. I pray for the light of God to shine in Man's ignorance in the body of Christ.
34. I pray that God will raise up intercessors.
35. I pray for the Word of God to be preached with signs and wonders.
36. I pray for God's Kingdom to come and His will to be done in churches across the world.
37. I pray for strongholds to come down among the believers.
38. I pray for God to have mercy and forgive us in areas where we come short.
39. I pray for mankind to be loosed from the bonds of wickedness, yolks to be broken, and heavy burdens to be lifted.
40. I pray for God's people, Israel, to receive salvation, and for His will to be done in this season of their lives.

Declarations and Decrees

1. God has not given me a spirit of fear, but of power, love, and a sound mind. (2 Timothy 1:7)
2. Surely the Lord will deliver me from the snare of the enemy and from pestilence. (Psalm 91:3)
3. I will not be afraid of the terror at night, nor from the arrows that fly in the daytime. (Psalm 91:5)
4. The Lord is my shepherd, and I will not lack for anything. (Psalm 23:1)
5. The Lord is my light and my salvation. I will not fear the enemy. (Psalm 27:1)
6. I have been blessed with spiritual blessings in heavenly places in Christ Jesus. (Ephesians 1:3)
7. By Jesus' stripes, I am healed. (Isaiah 53:5)
8. I am preserved in Christ Jesus. (Jude 1:1)
9. I receive the Word of God, which is health to my flesh. (Proverbs 4:22)
10. I seek first the Kingdom of God and His righteousness, and all things are added onto me. (Matthew 6:33)

Conclusion

THE CHRISTIAN LIFE is a continuous journey of getting to know Jesus Christ. The better acquainted we become with Him, the more we become like Him. We must be intentional about our spiritual growth and take responsibility. Speak into your life using the Word of God. Say what God says about you. Take authority over your situation, and don't leave it to others. Live by the values of the Word of God. Let prayer become a habit. When there is an attack on your spiritual life, take it seriously. You don't have to pray and ask whether or not it's an attack. KNOW that it is an attack. Pray.

As you hunger for God in your new life with Christ, please be aware that as you pray and fast, you will be opened to the spiritual world. When you are prophetic by nature, you can experience spiritual encounters. Spiritual encounters are the experiences that make the principles of the spiritual realm real in a believer's life. The devil wants to hijack your faith in God when you are at a vulnerable place in your spiritual growth with Christ. Believer's must be equipped and built up with the Word of God. Encounters are not equal to doctrine. We can't make doctrine out of encounters. Every encounter must submit to the scripture.

Get to know the person and ministry of the Holy Spirit. Get to know the person of the Lord Jesus Christ. Knowing the Trinity will keep you grounded and keep you from going astray from biblical doctrine. The Bible provides a road map to profitable spiritual encounters. Scripture must become your lens for interpreting your encounters.

The Holy Spirit is not the only spirit who has information about the spiritual realm. We are not wrestling with flesh and blood, but rather against spirits without bodies. If the devil can tempt Jesus, we are no match for him. It is very important to allow the Holy Spirit to guide you into all truth, or you can be easily led astray by other spirits. Just because someone can operate in the gifts, doesn't mean that they are in the Kingdom of God. The enemy has power too. What he does not have is authority in Christ.

Guard yourself from false prophets. Jesus said, "Beware of false prophets, which come to you in sheep's clothing, but inwardly they are ravening wolves."[159] Know the person who is laying hands on you or speaking into your life. People can transfer spirits, and you can find yourself under demonic influence.

Be aware that not every person who says they are a Christian or who is in the House of God is a child of God. Look for their fruit, not their gifts. Jesus said, "You will know them by their fruits."[160] The gifts are given, but

---

159 Matthew 7:15 (KJV)
160 Matthew 7:16 (NKJV)

the fruit comes because you are abiding in a relationship with Christ.

This is my testimony. Through pain and hardship, I came to understand these biblical truths. I thank God for His grace and mercy that brought me through. If it was not for His grace and mercy, I would not be writing this book now. My faith is stronger because of it.

Prayer is the hand that holds the key. The key is the faith that opens every door. Which door would you like to open? Remember, all blessings come from God to Mankind, but Men bless other Men. We need favor from God and from Man. The Word of God abides forever. It is the only guarantee that will never change. Continue in prayer… always.

About the Author

REVEREND SHARON DUNN has been in the ministry for 34 years and has been a youth pastor, a district leader, and a speaker in the Word of God. She has a Masters in Bible Theology. She has a passion for the Word of God and the people of God. Her inspiration comes from the love of God, and loving the people of God. She is a mother of four and grandmother of five.

CPSIA information can be obtained
at www.ICGtesting.com
Printed in the USA
LVHW071509170623
749831LV00002B/10